MARKETING YOUR SERVICE

MARKETING YOUR SERVICE

Jean Withers
Carol Vipperman

Self-Counsel Press
(a division of)
International Self-Counsel Press Ltd.
U.S.A. Canada

Printed in Canada.

First edition: 1987
Second edition: 1992; Reprinted: 1993
Third edition: 1998
Fourth edition: 2003

Canadian Cataloguing in Publication Data

Withers, Jean, 1944 -
  Marketing your service / Jean Withers, Carol Vipperman. — 4th ed.

  (Self-counsel business series)
  Previous ed. has title: Marketing your service business.
  ISBN 1-55180-395-X

  1. Service industries — Marketing. 2. Small business. I. Vipperman, Carol.
II. Title. III. Series.
HF5415.W58 2003   658.8   C2003-910051-0

Self-Counsel Press
(a division of)
International Self-Counsel Press Ltd.

1704 N. State Street
Bellingham, WA 98225
U.S.A.

1481 Charlotte Road
North Vancouver, BC V7J 1H1
Canada

To John and Jerry,
to their children,
and to our valued clients.

Thank you all for enriching our lives.

CONTENTS

TABLES

SAMPLES

WORKSHEETS

INTRODUCTION TO SERVICE MARKETING

The term *marketing* has a variety of meanings, each with a different connotation. Its most common meaning comes from the 1950s when manufacturers began to aggressively promote their products in all media — billboards, magazines, newspapers, radio, and television. Thus, for many people, marketing means advertisements, direct sales, direct mail, image creation, and public relations.

To many service providers, marketing seems commercial and, therefore, less than professional. Some service providers believe that if they begin active marketing, somehow they'll end up acting like hucksters on television. Furthermore, many service providers have tried the traditional marketing methods of the 1950s with frustration and without success.

Owners of service businesses and professional practices have realistic concerns about marketing. But in recent years changing rules, regulations, and expectations have removed the ethical concerns that restrained the professional world from marketing. It may now be acceptable for service providers to market, but many professionals still have difficulty adjusting their beliefs about marketing.

a. THE REAL DEFINITION OF MARKETING

Marketing is the activities that take your service from you to your client. Marketing is not simply advertising or public relations. It involves doing market research, analyzing your potential, setting goals and objectives, then using persuasive communication (which might include advertising and public relations) to sell your service.

A practical view of marketing is that of marketing strategy consultant Chuck Heinrich. He defines marketing as "the process of helping others value your service." In other words, marketing is what you and your staff do daily to help your clientele appreciate what you can do for them and how you do it. Marketing creates value in the minds of your clientele.

b. HOW SERVICE MARKETING DIFFERS FROM OTHER MARKETING

The ways service providers help clients value them are significantly different from the ways of other industries. For example, retailers depend on marketing to reach as many people as possible, whether customers are located in a particular geographical area or make up a particular interest group seeking the store's specialty. As a result, retailers use mass market techniques, direct mail, and in-store promotions.

But if you're like many service businesses and professional practices, broad, mass market techniques will not be effective. You have a specific market; therefore, a targeted approach and more personal contact are better suited to your marketing plan.

As well, the service you are marketing differs from retail goods because it is intangible. When clients use your service they buy only a promise that you'll deliver what you say you'll deliver. Your challenge is to market that promise so it is tangible to your clientele.

Just as retail marketing differs from service marketing, corporate marketing is different again. Corporations operate on highly structured marketing plans. In the corporate world, whole departments devote themselves to developing detailed marketing plans that use plentiful resources: a budget for promotion, sales seminars and marketing materials, and a number of people to implement the plans.

In contrast, service providers must actively market to clients helping them value the service) while actually delivering the service. They must constantly juggle getting the work, doing the work, and holding down the fort. As a consequence, marketing is not done consistently, which creates peaks and valleys of work.

c. MARKETING: ART AND SCIENCE

Oddly enough, when marketing is consistent, and when you develop marketing skill and experience, your workload will even out. Then you'll see what marketing really is: not huckster promotion, but both an art and a science. As a science it involves planning, analyzing, and discipline. As an art, it involves insight and creativity. Both art and science are inspired by the unparalleled strengths of your firm and its people.

To guide this process of marketing, you need a marketing plan. The plan will help guide your choices of how to market yourself, and the process of developing a plan will reveal an incredible amount of information about what your firm can offer to clients. In turn, your marketing plan can inspire your staff. For example, one firm found that as they involved more people in the process of developing the plan, their employees, including the receptionist, became more motivated. Each realized the important role to be played in helping clients value the firm and its services. And each then made a personal commitment to implementing the marketing plan.

The purpose of this book is to help you prepare a practical, effective marketing plan that responds to your marketplace and your needs. We hope to demystify marketing so you and your staff will understand that marketing is a part of what you do every day: it helps clients value your service so they remain clients and refer others. The procedures described in this book are useful and important for service businesses of all kinds:

Accountants
Actuarial practices
Advertising agencies
Appraisers
Architectural firms
Auto repair shops
Beauty salons

Business consultants
Chiropractors
Cleaners
Clinics
Color consultants
Computer consultants
Counselors
Court reporters
Delivery services
Dental practices
Desktop publishing
Engineering firms
Financial planners
Graphic designers
Health clubs
Home-based businesses
Hypnotherapists
Interior designers
Internet service providers
Investment advisory services
Janitorial services
Landscape architects
Landscape contractors

Lawyers
Massage therapists
Medical associations
Medical practices
Mental health services
Naturopathic physicians
Nutritionists
Optometrists
Personnel consultants
Photographers
Physicians
Printers
Psychologists
Rehabilitation services
Sales
Schools
Secretarial services
Tax preparers
Veterinarians
Web site designers
Wedding consultants
Word processing services
Writers

2
PREPARING YOUR ORGANIZATION FOR MARKETING

Your service business or professional practice may be new to marketing. If so, preparing your firm to begin marketing is as crucial as preparing the marketing plan. The difference between a masterful plan that fails and a pedestrian plan that succeeds can be your employees.

Since the need for change is usually seen at the top level of most businesses, it will require all your resolve and that of your associates to set your firm on the path to good marketing. Then you must see that it stays on that path. To guide your employees, follow *the three C's* of service marketing:

- Communication
- Change (and its impact on individuals)
- Coordination

If yours is a one-person firm, you obviously have only yourself to prepare.

a. COMMUNICATION

Because the partners in a firm often see the need for marketing, they may assume that others in the firm see it as well. In fact, this is rarely true. Some partners believe that marketing can take place at the top without involving employees. This might be possible in industries such as manufacturing where employees rarely interact directly with customers. But in service businesses with intelligent, well-educated employees who often have more contact with the clients than management does, "marketing at the top" is ill-advised.

Include your employees in your marketing planning effort as soon as it gets underway. If this is the first time your firm has developed a plan, explain why it is important. Because of the ethical concerns discussed earlier, some professionals will view marketing negatively and will need to be told both the benefits of developing a plan and the consequences of not developing one. Stress how imperative their assistance is and explain that their perspective, which may be quite different from management's, is invaluable and irreplaceable. Let them know that marketing simply cannot succeed without their enthusiastic support.

Continue to involve employees throughout development of the marketing plan. They can provide information for the marketing effort, so ask different employees for information as needed. Ask their opinions about client relations,

4

for example. Communicate your philosophy for acquiring, maintaining, and retaining clients. As you discuss it, your employees will come to understand the image you want to project to clients, the way you want complaints handled, and so on. The interaction will be helpful as an old planning adage predicts: the plan may be worthless, but the process is invaluable.

After the plan is developed and implementation begins, your employees' enthusiasm and support will be directly related to the amount of information and feedback they receive. They will wonder which marketing projects are scheduled to begin soon and whether or not the company is achieving its goals. Communicate the answers, perhaps in an internal company newsletter or bulletin as many firms do. Or, hold meetings on a monthly or quarterly basis; at these meetings, update your employees about the progress of the marketing plan.

Giving your employees a way to give you feedback is equally important, both for the useful information and the motivation it will provide. You'll want to ask employees to contribute their observations and relay customer comments that relate to the marketing plan.

b. CHANGE (AND INDIVIDUALS)

In addition to considering the impact of marketing on them as a group, employees, partners, and associates in your firm should be aware of what the marketing plan means to them individually. In smaller firms, a group meeting may suffice. In larger firms, or in those that previously have not expected employees to become involved in marketing, you may want to discuss marketing with each person.

First discuss the firm's expectations of his or her role with each employee. Explain why change is needed. For example, a lawyer who delivers quality legal work will need to understand why marketing must be added to day-to-day activities. Be prepared to discuss how he or she might acquire the skills to do the marketing job (e.g., through a training program).

What kinds of results are you expecting from that person? Explain this in terms of specific behavior and activity. Don't say, "I want you to bring in more business" or "I want you to be a contributing member of the firm in our marketing efforts." Define what you mean; make sure the individual understands what it takes to become "a contributing member." Say, for example, "I expect you to invite one key client a week to lunch for the purpose of solidifying relationships and developing referrals."

Be prepared for some resistance. Technical employees are usually the most likely to resist marketing. When you meet resistance, recognize it as normal and consider additional assistance or communication that might help such employees overcome their discomfort. Try to understand why they are resisting, and help them see why marketing is necessary or desirable.

Then make certain everyone has the same meaning for marketing terms such as *business development*, *client retention*, or *client recruitment*. Plan marketing training very soon. Your employees, who will become salespeople, *must* have training tailored to selling a service. If your company does not have training resources, consider bringing in a consultant to train members of your firm. Send key personnel (including yourself) to a sales training course. Whatever your decision, your employees'

Results: Melissa consistant comm with Hiba. ie time + X. Order TX is needed. Explain to her clearly.

Hiba. 80% retention of Hyg + 85% of new TX

5

confidence and comfort in marketing depends on both knowing what they're doing and being able to identify with the role. They must recognize that marketing and service are *not* mutually exclusive.

c. COORDINATION

Before you implement your marketing plan, appoint someone to coordinate the marketing effort. As the service provider, you may do it, or the coordinator might be another individual or a committee.

The role of the coordinator or coordinating team is to ensure that, once the plan has been developed, the momentum persists throughout implementation. The coordinator also motivates your employees and assures them that the firm is moving ahead through marketing.

Some firms offer a monetary reward for marketing efforts, such as a percentage of sales and profits, or, as in some larger professional firms, a percentage of sales only. Other firms rely on recognition alone. Build incentives into your system to help encourage marketing before you implement the marketing plan.

Take time to prepare your firm for marketing. It will lead to a more productive and successful marketing program.

DEVELOPING A MARKETING PLAN 3

A marketing plan is a working document you and others in your service business or professional practice will use and review on an ongoing basis. It is not an abstract treatise you develop and then put on the shelf. A marketing plan is meant to be used to measure how you are doing, where you have been, and what needs to be done differently in the future. It is not cast in concrete when written, but is a flexible working document. Most marketing plans are revised annually. Your service business or professional practice may change more quickly, generating a need to supplement it quarterly or semiannually with more specific action plans.

a. WHERE ARE YOU NOW?

The answers to three questions make up a marketing plan. The first question is, "Where are you now?" Answering this question creates the most intensive phase of the marketing process. You must assess your firm internally and externally. Look at the mission, or purpose, of the business:

- Where are you headed?
- What are your services?
- Which services are more viable or competitive than others?

Services: ortho - hyg council
6 mth hyg.

- What fees do you charge?
- What are your resources?

The last question is critical for service businesses and professional practices because the raw materials available to make the firm grow and succeed are the firm's personnel or, in many cases, just the service provider. What are the strengths and weaknesses of your personnel? What skills or areas of knowledge need to be strengthened?

In addition to looking inside your business, it is essential to analyze the external marketplace:

- Who is your clientele?
- Who is the competition?
- How is your business different?
- What problems emerge?
- What opportunities do you see ahead?
- What are the trends in your service business or profession?

All of this will help you understand where you are now and what is actually happening in the marketplace more clearly. Then you will be prepared to ask the second question.

b. WHERE DO YOU WANT TO BE?

Where do you want to be as a firm? What kind of image do you want? What kind of income? What kind of service? Answers to these questions form the basis of your goals and your objectives and the core of your marketing plan. Think clearly!

Consultants to service businesses and professional practices often feel like the Cheshire cat in *Alice's Adventures in Wonderland*. Alice comes upon the cat, which is sitting in a tree; the cat is smiling, as many consultants do. In front of Alice are three paths. She asks the cat, "Which path should I take?" The cat, smiling, looks at her and says, "Well, where would you like to go?" Alice says, "I don't know." The cat responds, "Then any path will take you there."

In service marketing, this is especially true. Any marketing technique and any promotional strategy discussed in this book will take you somewhere. Only you can decide where you want to go.

c. HOW DO YOU GET THERE?

The final question is, "How do you get there?" The answer to this question probably prompted many of you to read this book. The decisions made about your goals and objectives will determine your answer.

This question addresses your target markets — the clientele you plan to serve — and determines the most effective strategies for your services, fees, distribution, and promotion.

To answer the question, you need to write down every action and every step you will take, in order, and coordinate each with the other. Finally, you need to develop a system to monitor the effect of the strategies you've developed. It will give you the feedback necessary for success.

The rest of the book explains the specific steps to take to develop and write your marketing action plan.

STATING YOUR COMPANY MISSION 4

a. WHY HAVE A MISSION STATEMENT?

Every service business and professional practice has a purpose. It might be the reason you started your business. It could be the reason you're in business now. Or it could be what you want your business to become.

Stating your purpose for being, your company mission, at the beginning of your marketing plan helps you focus your energy as you prepare and implement your plan. It orients you to the primary purpose of your business, and it helps you make decisions directed toward accomplishing that purpose. The clearer your vision, the easier it is to see marketing opportunities and respond to them successfully. A purpose that is unclear or one-dimensional (e.g., "to make money" or "be creative") is difficult to keep in focus and communicate to others.

b. WHAT IS A MISSION STATEMENT, ANYWAY?

Simply defined, your mission statement is 25 words that summarize your organization's purpose for being. Writing those 25 words may be easy if you, as the service provider, see your mission shining clear as a beacon. Or, writing your mission

statement may be extremely difficult if three partners see three different beacons and even if you, as a single owner, have never clarified the purpose of your business.

In the case of a one-owner housecleaning service with a clear purpose, the mission statement might read: "To provide quality, personalized housecleaning services so that I enhance my clients' quality of life (through more free time, more relaxation, and less stress)."

With several partners and as many missions, clarification and compromise are required. Each person's expectations, preferences, and perceptions must be discussed honestly and with respect. For example, one partner in a law firm whose mission is to provide lower-income clients with a wide spectrum of legal services will need to listen closely to the partner whose mission is to actively solicit business from major corporations, and to the third partner whose mission is to provide estate planning assistance to upper-income individuals. Each partner must listen carefully to the other's primary purpose for being in business.

The admirable qualities of listening and understanding, however, can be a double-edged sword in business. First, too much time spent discussing *anything* produces

9

no revenue. Second, for any business to succeed, astute business judgment *must* prevail. Compromise among the purposes of each partner must lead to the best choice for the service business or professional practice as a whole.

When a service provider operates independently and without a clear sense of what services are to be provided to whom, he or she has a greater challenge: self-examination, followed by focusing. Choosing the services to be provided and the clients to be served implies choosing the services and clients to be eliminated — which you may find alarming. Yet everyone who buys a service responds best when the purpose is clear.

c. HOW DO YOU DEVELOP THE MISSION STATEMENT?

Any self-respecting mission statement should include the following:

- The needs your company fulfills
- Clients you serve now or want to serve
- How you will go about serving these clients (e.g., through consultation)
- The service business your firm is in

Your statement should be broad rather than specific. A hundred years ago, railroad magnates erred by limiting themselves to the "railroad" business rather than thinking of themselves as being in the "transportation" business. Had they seen the broader picture of moving goods by land, sea, and air, they would also have seen the greater opportunity.

In addition, your mission statement should be positive and forceful. If your beacon is a bright one, you'll want your mission statement to reflect its light. For example, "to help mid-sized companies achieve their goals through critical training and human resources consultation" is a more powerful image than "to consult with companies on personnel, training, and management issues."

The mission statement should also be free of jargon. How safe and secure it feels to wrap a statement in language only a few understand. But how obscure and frustrating such a statement is to others — including those you want to serve.

You may choose to depersonalize the statement to emphasize "the firm" or "the company" more than an individual. Regardless, limiting the statement to no more than 25 words assures conciseness.

d. FIND THE MISSING MISSION STATEMENT

To illustrate the process of developing a mission statement, consider this example of a rather simple service business:

Imagine that you are the owner of Case Inc., a consulting firm that helps businesses with no in-house training departments train new employees. You began your partnership 3 years ago after 20 years' experience in education and government. Your consulting firm now employs two people who provide clerical support and technical support to the firm's projects.

You customize your consulting service to the needs of each client and pride yourself on cost-effective, behavior-oriented practical skills. For your service, you charge a flat fee calculated monthly. This, too, is a unique approach, different from the competition.

Your office is located downtown in a metropolitan center. You have tried several techniques to promote your business, including seminars, brochures, and direct sales calls. You consider yourself to be an average promoter. Your staff is excellent in their technical abilities and good with clients. Your clients tend to be mid-sized firms. In the first three years of business, you made $75,000 in consultation fees. One of your concerns about your income is the lack of profit due to the number of people-hours required for each job.

There are many trainers who provide the same service in your city, but few who operate in this manner. You think that you are creative and better able to focus on the big picture and on results needed by clients. You suspect that in the future your concept of delivering services will be more acceptable and also that clients will grow and add their own training departments (thus throwing you out of a job).

With that information, how would you write the mission statement of this business? To do so, *don't* begin by struggling to find the proper words. Just skim the example again and jot down a few ideas. Pause before evaluating your list of ideas. Now, cross off those ideas that don't seem important on second reading and check off those that do. Read your revised list of important ideas and turn that piece of paper over. Now, very quickly, write three or four sentences explaining the purpose of that business.

Pause. Look away. Read your sentences again aloud. How did you do? If you're like most writers, you'll need to edit. Remember, clarity, positiveness, and forcefulness are important. Write your final mission statement in the space provided.

MISSION STATEMENT OF CASE INC.

_____

_____

_____

_____

_____

_____

_____

_____

_____

_____

How about it? Would you hire a firm with a mission statement like that? If not, compare it to the sample statement below. You might want to rework your version. However, we suggest you save your energy for your own mission statement. Use Worksheet #1 to write your statement.

SAMPLE #1
CASE INC. MISSION STATEMENT

To provide counseling and consulting services to individuals and organizations in the area of stress management and communication.

WORKSHEET #1
MISSION STATEMENT

PART I

Whether you've owned your service business or professional practice for years or are just starting:

1. What business do you want to be in?

_____

_____

_____

_____

2. What needs do you wish to serve?

_____

_____

_____

_____

3. What clients do you want to serve?

_____

_____

_____

_____

4. How will you go about this task (e.g., for an auto repair shop, through consulting and service, not through sales calls or advertising)?

_____

_____

_____

_____

PART 2

COMPANY MISSION STATEMENT

In 25 words or less, state your company's mission.

_____

_____

_____

_____

_____

_____

_____

_____

_____

_____

_____

_____

_____

_____

_____

_____

_____

_____

_____

_____

_____

_____

_____

_____

GATHERING THE FACTS ABOUT YOUR BUSINESS

a. THE BASIS FOR YOUR MARKETING PLAN

Any business plan begins with the present. For example, to plan financially, you first determine what cash and financial resources are available. To plan an increased work effort, you first assess staff talents and experience. To plan marketing, you first look inside your service business or professional practice.

An in-depth look inside your service business or professional practice will help you assess six aspects of your firm:

- The service you offer (product)
- Where you offer that service, or the way you offer it (place)
- The fees you charge (price),
- How you promote your service to clients (promotion)
- Your clients, and sales of your service

The first four aspects of your business are the classic "Four P's of Marketing": product, place, price, and promotion (interpreted for service businesses). The last two aspects are the lifeblood of your company: clients and the sales your services to them generate. Assessing your service business or professional practice in all its parts will provide a solid foundation of facts on which you, your partners, and your staff can build both the marketing plan and future business.

b. ASSESSING YOUR SERVICES

Yes, yes. You know what services your firm offers. For example, as an accountant, you offer financial advice, record keeping, and monthly statements. As a hair stylist, you provide hair cuts, coloring, and permanents. Yet few service providers see their services as their clients or prospective clients see them. You must translate your service into the terms of the marketplace.

Marketing planning helps you see your service from your clients' perspective and may be a real challenge to service providers. You may be very familiar with what you do and how you do it. You may take great pride in your work, your skills, and your years of experience because you see how significantly you can influence a client's life. You may be very familiar with what, in marketing language, are called the *features* of your service. You may be less familiar with what your clients get out of your service, or, its *benefits*.

Generally, describing features is easy, but identifying benefits is confusing and difficult. Benefits (or *results* if that word is more descriptive for you) might be defined by imagining your clients saying, "What's in it for me?" or "What do I get out of it?" For example, a presentation skills educator might identify providing videotaping services during seminars as a feature. As a result, seminar participants receive more than just videotaped presentations. They see their current speaking habits, recognize their errors, and improve rapidly — a clear benefit.

The words describing a benefit should be simple, nontechnical, and emotionally powerful. If such marketing words don't come easily to you, sit down with an intelligent but uninformed friend or with less technical staff members. Ask, "If I said this is a feature of a service I'm providing, and you used the service, what would you get out of it?"

Use Worksheet #2 to analyze and summarize your services.

c. DISTRIBUTING YOUR SERVICE: ITS PLACE

In marketing, *place* means not only a physical space but also the way your service business or professional practice offers its service. For example, to real estate appraisers, place is both the office (the physical space) and the practice of going to residences to make appraisals (the way service is distributed).

Assess your company's place on Worksheet #3. Remember to see your place through the eyes of your customers, the marketing perspective established to assess your services in Worksheet #2. Then summarize what you've discovered.

d. EVALUATING PRICES AND FEES

Prices and fees often seem simple. For example, an auto-rebuild business charges set prices for labor, body work, and painting. A lawyer charges set fees for each billable hour. But the art of pricing is more complex than that. It includes not only what fees are charged, but how they are paid. Credit offered to clients and the basis for offering it are issues to be considered, as are how often and when to change fees. And what about those extra, unanticipated, or customized services?

In addition, formal pricing rules do not exist for many service businesses. Thus, each service provider must set his or her own fees — a difficult task without experience. Typically, individuals new to business underprice others offering the same service. While underpricing helps build their client base, it has continually been shown to also cause clients to undervalue their service. Service providers who underprice are unable to offer quality services and still make a living. Their per hour rate is too low to afford them the time to achieve excellence and still eat. By setting fees low, they undermine not only others but themselves.

It is essential to know what others in the same field charge for similar services. This information may be difficult to obtain if your competition refuses to assist you. If so, you might consider one of these strategies:

- Call, describe yourself as a prospective client, and ask what the fees would be.

- Hire someone to make such calls for you.
- Use the services of a competitor.
- Ask a local expert in your field about pricing.
- Ask a professional or trade association about fees.

To aid you in thinking through your fees, complete Worksheet #4 and summarize your findings.

e. TELLING THE WORLD ABOUT YOUR SERVICE

Over the years, you may have tried to inform prospective clients about your service business or professional practice in a number of ways. You might have taken out advertisements in publications or in the Yellow Pages. You might have produced brochures. Your service business might have been featured in a newspaper article or on radio or television. You might have published an article. Friends and colleagues might have referred a client to you.

To assess the effectiveness of what you've done to promote your service and to learn new techniques, Worksheet #5 will be helpful. However, be aware of three factors as you complete it. First, accept that promotion is one of the most complex aspects of marketing.

Second, realize that marketing professional services is a new discipline. You are a pioneer traveling over rough and uncertain roads when you practice it. Don't let obstacles frustrate or overwhelm you. Instead, enjoy the lessons you'll learn.

Third, know that the effectiveness of even the best and most professional marketing campaign is often difficult to measure. Generally, service providers feel disappointed with their promotional efforts — in part because they give up too soon. Look for this pattern as you review your firm's efforts.

Fill out Worksheet #5, then summarize what you've learned.

f. KNOW THY CLIENT

1. Importance of each client

As a rule, service businesses are proportionally smaller than other kinds of businesses, such as manufacturing. Also, service businesses and professional practices are part of highly fragmented industries. Architecture, for example, is made up of small groups of architects often working in isolation from one another. Each firm can service only a small number of clients, so each client is proportionally more important to the firm than he or she would be to large industry.

Because each client is so important, professional practices and other service businesses must know, in precise detail, who they are serving. Such knowledge is fundamental, not just to surviving, but to thriving in a service business.

To know your clients well requires several types of information. Some information is easily available; other information has to be collected. Although you will ultimately generalize about your clients, during the process of identifying them you will develop a more personal and profound sense of their needs.

First, analyze your clients to determine what characteristics they share. One of hundreds of old adages about sales holds true: Identify five common characteristics of your past clients and you'll be able to see the next one walking down the street. You will also see trends that will help you identify how to reach current and future customers.

Second, find out how frequently your clients use your service. How much do they buy? When? This is a particularly vital issue for service providers to understand. Often there are opportunities to increase client patronage that you are not aware of now. For example, one law firm learned that, after they incorporated a small business, officers of the corporation often failed to hold legally required annual meetings. The law firm realized they could provide a valuable service and increase billable hours by simply scheduling such meetings for corporate officers in their office.

Worksheet #6 will help you learn about your clients and their past need for you.

2. If you don't know your clients

If you've found it difficult or impossible to complete the previous worksheets, you're not alone. No matter how important clients are, few service providers know enough about them.

To learn more, check the information that is available to you, what marketers call *primary sources:*

- *You already know some information about your clients.* If you're sure it is correct, use the information you already have. Just remember that much of your marketing plan will be based on it and erroneous assumptions now could lead you down the wrong marketing path later.
- *Pull information from client records.* You may have considerable information already collected in client

files. Addresses, for example, might give you insight into important client characteristics. Don't expect this information to be organized in a way that makes marketing easy. Also, files may not be complete, so if your firm has a high sales volume and many clients, refer to lists of clients; it's likely you'll forget somebody if you don't.

- *Conduct a customer survey.* Some information may be lacking after you and your associates have provided what you already know and you have researched client files. If so, ask your clients for such information, in this case, through a survey. Choose a telephone survey (which is fast but expensive), a mail questionnaire (which can be more extensive but result in fewer responses), or an in-person survey. Clients might complete a survey (no more than one-and-a-half pages long) when they come to your place of business. Or, you might hire a researcher to interview them, or ask questions yourself.

In an in-person survey, ask about things you're not sure of. Ask what clients like or don't like about the service (clients answer this question more easily when a researcher, rather than you, asks them). Ask the questions objectively, and ask less sensitive questions first and more sensitive questions later (e.g., questions about income). Give clients the opportunity to be anonymous. If you conduct the survey at your location, ask clients to fill it out while their bill is being calculated and provide a box clearly marked "client surveys" on the sales counter or at the receptionist's desk.

Send self-addressed, stamped envelopes if you mail questionnaires.

The types of questions you ask can vary depending on the way you administer the questionnaire (telephone, mail, or in-person). See Table #1.

To learn more about your clients, check information that someone else collects and publishes, what is called *secondary information*. Governments, banks, major city newspapers, and international sales and marketing organizations all publish information that can be useful to you. Ask the librarians in the business department of your public or university libraries for resources that could be helpful to you. And don't forget the Internet; there is a wealth of information on the Web if you know what you are looking for.

For example, a residential and commercial upholstery and rug cleaning service, using updated census data available through a government Web site, found that a growing number of older, higher income families were moving into its market area. Owners were able to adapt their marketing plan to this group.

Before it can be useful to you, though, information from secondary sources must meet the following tests:

- *It must be local.* The information must be relevant to your geographical area and to the population you serve. Such information is a particular problem for services with a small customer base.

- *It must be accurate.* An additional problem regarding data drawn from a small area is that the smaller the sample surveyed, the less the degree of accuracy. The only reasonable choice is to assume that it is accurate if it has passed the test of being published.

- *It must be timely.* As change in our society accelerates, up-to-date data may be hard to find. A changing population and changing trends are increasingly difficult to track.

Secondary sources are constantly refining their methods for collecting information. Therefore, the data you need may well be available locally. In addition, the growing use of the Internet has encouraged more frequent data updating, so up-to-date information is more easily available.

3. If your business has no customers yet

If your service business or professional practice is new, choosing the clients you want to serve will be one of your most important decisions.

Use the survey techniques previously described, but talk to experts who know both the service you provide and the clientele you wish to serve. Also talk to individuals or businesses like those you want to serve. Organize an unpaid volunteer board of advisers to refine your ideas.

4. Customer communications and service

Think about it for a moment. How well does your company handle the small, but significant, details of everyday business? How rapidly and how cordially is the telephone answered? How well are letters typed? How promptly are calls returned? Even more important, what is the image of your company? How well is your business or professional practice presented?

TABLE #1
QUESTIONS FOR CLIENT QUESTIONNAIRES

Type	Description	Examples	Advantages	Disadvantages
Open-ended question	Respondents are free to reply to open-ended questions in their own words rather than being limited to choosing from a set of alternatives.	What types of services do you normally use? What in particular do you value in the service XYZ firm provides?	• Provides quick answers • Generally little misunderstanding in explaining questions • Can elicit in-depth information	• May be hard to summarize answers • Difficult to record and interpret answers accurately
Multiple choice question	The multiple choice question is a fixed alternative question. That is, respondents are asked to choose the alternatives that most closely correspond to their positions on a subject.	How old are you? ___20 or younger ___20 – 29 ___30 – 39 ___40 – 49 ___50 or older	• If constructed properly, lists all possible relevant alternatives • Orderly and systematic • Less demanding of interviewer • Lower cost • Easily tabulated and analyzed	• Presupposes you know all relevant alternative answers • May not present alternatives clearly • Choices may have different meanings for different respondents • Order of choices may bias answers
Dual choice question	The dual choice question is also a fixed alternative question, but one in which only two alternatives are listed. These may be "yes/no" or "true/false" alternatives.	Are you the person in your firm who makes the decision about contracting service? ___ Yes ___ No	• Provides a specific answer that is quickly tabulated and analyzed • Relatively easy to answer • Orderly and systematic • Less demanding of interviewer • Good lead-in to more detailed questions	• Forces respondent to make a choice, even though he or she might be uncertain • Provides no detailed information • Difficult to word properly
Rating scale	Scales can be used to capture the intensity of responses.	How would you rate the quality of our service? ___very good ___good ___average ___poor	• Measures intensity of feelings toward an issue	• Scale intervals may not be distinct in respondent's mind • Scale intervals may not reflect respondent's knowledge levels • Respondent may interpret terms differently (e.g., what "average" means)

To find out, answer the questions on Worksheet #7.

g. WHAT HAVE YOU SOLD RECENTLY?

Sales are the lifeblood of any business. An intensive, in-depth look at how much of what services has been sold will help you understand what your clients need and buy. Comparing this year's sales figures with those of past years will help you understand how rapidly your service business or professional practice is growing.

Assessing the number and percentage of new clients may be encouraging as well.

In addition to just knowing the sales figures, knowing who purchased, which service was purchased, and what size sale (large, medium, small) was made is almost always valuable. As well, knowing where the sale was made, that is, analyzing sales by geographical area, has caused businesses to make dramatic business decisions.

Use Worksheet #8 to analyze the sales of your service.

Name of each service:

How you provide the service:

_____
_____
_____
_____
_____
_____
_____
_____
_____
_____
_____

_____
_____
_____
_____
_____
_____
_____
_____
_____
_____
_____

Features of the service (What is it?):

Benefits of the service (What's in it for your clients? Why should they buy?):

_____
_____
_____
_____
_____
_____
_____
_____
_____

_____
_____
_____
_____
_____
_____
_____
_____
_____

WORKSHEET #2 — Continued

	Very Good	Good	Average	Poor	Comments
1. Are your services of good quality?					
2. How safe are your services?					
3. How well do your services deliver what your business promises?					
4. Do the names of your services really communicate the benefit your clients will receive?					

5. If your business offers more than one service, are they compatible (e.g., it would be incongruous for IBM to sell ice cream bars)?

❑ Yes   ❑ No

Comments:_____

_____

6. Does your business have the equipment necessary to offer the service (e.g., computer layout programs in a printing firm)?

❑ Yes   ❑ No

Comments:_____

_____

7. Does your business have the necessary materials, or can it get them easily (e.g., cloth for a clothing manufacturer)?

❑ Yes   ❑ No

Comments:_____

_____

8. In your opinion, where on the following service life cycle chart are the services your firm offers?

Maturity

Introduction   Decline

SERVICES SUMMARY

Summarize the characteristics of your services.

_____

_____

_____

_____

_____

_____

_____

_____

_____

_____

_____

_____

_____

WORKSHEET #3
THE PLACE OF YOUR SERVICE

1. From what premises does your business sell its service to clients?
   ❑ Office in a commercial building
   ❑ Office, studio, or shop in your home
   ❑ At customer's home or place of business
   ❑ Other (specify): _____

2. From how many outlets does your business sell its service?
   ❑ One   ❑ More than one

3. How did you decide on the number and location of your place(s) of business?

   Location   Reasons for selecting location

   _____

   _____

   _____

   _____

4. Does your place of business meet your requirements or are physical changes or improvements needed?
   ❑ Okay as is
   ❑ Physical changes needed (specify):_____

   _____

   _____

   _____

5. What would it cost to make such changes?

   Change   Expensive   Moderate   Inexpensive

   _____

   _____

   _____

6. If public access to your place of business is important, can your clients reach it easily?
    - ❑ Accessible to public transit   ❑ Accessible to customers' homes
    - ❑ Accessible to parking   ❑ Not applicable
    - ❑ Accessible to customers' offices

7. Are your firm's present premises a suitable size for your type of business?
    - ❑ Yes   ❑ No (specify size needed):_____

8. If not, can you feasibly do something about this?
    - ❑ Yes   ❑ No   ❑ Undecided

9. Will you have enough room at this location when your business grows?
    - ❑ Yes   ❑ No   ❑ Don't know

10. Will you need to expand into other outlets when the business grows?
    - ❑ Yes   ❑ No   ❑ Undecided

11. If you decide to expand, what criteria will you use in choosing the new location?

    _____

    _____

    _____

12. What will be the effect of making physical changes or improvements at your place of business?_____

    _____

    _____

13. What will be the effect of not making improvements? _____

    _____

    _____

14. Are there any feasible changes you can make to improve client access to your place(s) of business?

☐ No   ☐ Yes (describe:)

_____

_____

15. Are there changes you can make to better serve your clients?

☐ Sell your service some other way (e.g., provide training on cassette tapes)

☐ Consider offering your service over the Internet

☐ Consider building a "broker" referral network to sell your services

☐ Consider publishing books and pamphlets to better communicate and sell your services

☐ Consider putting your service on the road (e.g., a mobile diagnostic center for physicians or a mobile glass repair service)

_____

_____

_____

_____

_____

_____

_____

_____

_____

_____

_____

_____

_____

_____

_____

PLACE SUMMARY

Summarize the description you've developed about the place and way your business offers its service.

_____

_____

_____

_____

_____

_____

_____

_____

_____

_____

_____

_____

_____

_____

_____

_____

_____

_____

_____

_____

_____

_____

_____

_____

WORKSHEET #4
PRICING

1. What fees do you charge for your services?

   Service   Fee

   _____

   _____

   _____

2. Does your business accept cash (or check) only, or does it permit credit?

   ❑ Cash only   ❑ Credit

3. What credit terms does your business offer?

   ❑ Extended time (e.g., payments continue over terms of a year or more)

   ❑ Restricted time period (e.g., 30 days, 90 days)

   ❑ Other (specify): _____

4. What proportion of your sales are cash and what proportion are on credit?

   _____% cash sales annually

   _____% credit sales annually

5. What type of discounts does your business offer, if any?

   ❑ Cash discounts (to clients who pay bills within a specified period of time)

   ❑ Quantity discounts (to clients who purchase in quantity)

6. Does your business charge strictly for the service, or does it charge extra for special services?

   ❑ Charges only for the service

   ❑ Charges for travel

   ❑ Charges for client-related entertainment

   ❑ Levies other charges (specify):_____

7. When was the last time your business changed fees? _____

8. Did you increase or decrease fees?

❑ Increased fees ❑ Decreased fees

9. To the best of your knowledge, how do your clients perceive your fee?

❑ Expensive ❑ Moderate ❑ Inexpensive

10. To the best of your knowledge, are your fees competitive?

❑ Yes ❑ No ❑ Don't know

11. If your business does not currently charge for extra services, are there services the business provides for which an extra charge might be levied? How much might you charge?

_____

_____

_____

12. If you don't offer credit, do you think offering credit terms would provide an incentive to your clients to buy your service?

❑ Yes ❑ No ❑ Perhaps

13. Do you think fee changes are necessary?

Service   Increase? Decrease? Amount?

_____

_____

_____

14. How would your clients respond to such fee changes?

_____

_____

_____

15. Is such a change worth the response?

☐ Definitely   ☐ Possibly   ☐ Undecided

PRICE SUMMARY

Summarize the fee information you have developed.

_____

_____

_____

_____

_____

_____

_____

_____

_____

_____

_____

_____

_____

_____

_____

_____

_____

_____

_____

_____

_____

GENERAL PROMOTION INFORMATION

1. What efforts have you initiated to persuade people to purchase your service?
    - ❑ Sold directly to clients
    - ❑ Sought publicity in mass media (e.g., newspapers, radio, and television)
    - ❑ Advertised your service over the Internet
    - ❑ Spoke to professional organizations
    - ❑ Requested referrals from colleagues and previous clients
    - ❑ Mailed directly to clients
    - ❑ Offered sales promotions (e.g., samples, premiums, coupons, contests)
    - ❑ Advertised in publications
    - ❑ Other (specify): _____

2. How frequently have these promotional activities occurred?
    - ❑ Frequently
    - ❑ Sporadically
    - ❑ Not at all

3. If you offer more than one service, have you promoted each one?
    - ❑ Yes   ❑ No

    Explain: _____

    _____

    _____

    _____

    _____

    _____

    _____

    _____

    _____

    _____

    _____

DIRECT SALES EFFORTS

If you are the sole salesperson for your service business or professional practice:

1. How many direct sales calls do you make in a week?
   - ❏ 5 or fewer calls
   - ❏ 6 – 10 calls
   - ❏ 11 – 15 calls
   - ❏ More than 15 calls

2. Do you make in-person sales calls or telephone sales calls?
   - ❏ In-person
   - ❏ Telephone

3. How many hours do you spend selling per week? _____

4. Where do you get your sales leads?
   - ❏ Advertisements
   - ❏ Membership lists
   - ❏ Suggestions from colleagues
   - ❏ Yellow Pages
   - ❏ Other (specify): _____

5. How many sales (in numbers and in dollars) do you average per month? _____

6. Have you done any direct selling before in your career? Explain:_____
   _____
   _____
   _____

7. Have you received any sales training before?
   _____
   _____
   _____
   _____

8. In what aspect of your sales calls do you need the most help?
   - ❑ Getting leads
   - ❑ Asking questions that reveal client needs
   - ❑ Handling client objections
   - ❑ Closing the sales
   - ❑ Following up after the call (e.g., preparing the proposal)
   - ❑ Selling by phone
   - ❑ Getting motivated to sell
   - ❑ Other (specify): _____

If you manage a staff of salespeople:

1. How many salespeople are on your staff? _____

2. What are their sales responsibilities? _____

_____

_____

3. How are your business's salespeople paid?
   ❑ Salary   ❑ Salary plus commission   ❑ Commission

4. Is your sales staff large enough to adequately sell to and service your clients?
   ❑ Yes   ❑ No (How many additional salespeople are needed?)_____

5. Have your sales people had any sales training?
   ❑ Yes   ❑ No   ❑ Some

6. Has your business offered sales training for their jobs with your firm?
   ❑ Yes   ❑ No
   Explain: _____

_____

_____

_____

WORKSHEET #5 — Continued

7. Identify the strengths/weaknesses of your sales force.

_____

_____

_____

PUBLICITY EFFORTS

1. Has your business actively sought free publicity?
   ☐ Yes   ☐ No
   Explain: _____

   _____

   _____

2. If yes, in what media has your firm sought publicity?

   _____

   _____

   _____

3. Who initiated contact that generated publicity?
   ☐ Someone in the firm   ☐ A reporter

4. Did publicity efforts result in stories?
   ☐ Yes   ☐ No

5. What kinds of stories were written about your firm?

   _____

   _____

   _____

PUBLIC SPEAKING RECORD

1. Have you ever spoken to a group about your service?
   ❑ Yes   ❑ No

2. If not, would you or others in your business feel able to do so? _____

3. If so, what type of group did you or your associates speak to?
   ❑ Community organization
   ❑ Professional association
   ❑ Special interest group
   ❑ Social group
   ❑ Political group

4. Did you or your associates provide the audience with supplemental aids (such as a brochure or a sample) when you spoke?
   ❑ Yes   ❑ No
   Explain: _____

   _____

   _____

   _____

   _____

5. What was the impact of your speech?
   ❑ Considerable audience interest at the event
   ❑ One or more leads (prospective customers)
   ❑ New customers purchased the service
   ❑ No response

REFERRALS

1. Has your business received referrals of prospective clients from colleagues, past clients, or personal friends?

   ❑ Yes   ❑ No

2. Have you asked such people for referrals?

   ❑ Yes   ❑ No

   Explain: _____

   _____

   _____

3. Referrals are approximately what percentage of your total clients? _____

4. Do you routinely contact satisfied clients after a job is completed?

   _____

   _____

   _____

PARTICIPATION IN ORGANIZATIONS

1. What groups or professional associations are you or others in your business members of?

   _____

   _____

   _____

2. Why did you and your associates join these organizations?

   ❑ Support   ❑ Business leads

   ❑ Other reasons (specify): _____

3. How have you and your associates used your membership in these organizations to promote business?
   - ❏ Served as public spokesperson for organization
   - ❏ Served on committees or as executive officer
   - ❏ Told other members about my business
   - ❏ Asked for referrals from other members
   - ❏ Have not used membership for business development

4. How else might you and your associates encourage other people to refer prospective clients to you? _____
   _____
   _____
   _____

SALES PROMOTIONS

1. Have you used sales promotions as incentives to encourage clients to purchase your service?
   ❏ Yes   ❏ No
   Explain: _____
   _____
   _____

2. What kinds of sales promotion has your business used?
   - ❏ Trade shows
   - ❏ Free initial consultation
   - ❏ Lower fees
   - ❏ Included more staff at no extra fee
   - ❏ Seminars
   - ❏ Included books or tapes of work with no extra fee
   - ❏ Invited clients on trips or special evening out at ball game, symphony, etc.
   - ❏ Gimmicks (e.g., T-shirts for placing orders)

3. How frequently have you used such sales promotions?

_____

_____

_____

DIRECT MAIL EFFORTS

1. Have you used direct mail (e.g., mailing promotional brochures or flyers directly to homes or offices) to reach your clients?

❑ Yes   ❑ No

Explain: _____

_____

_____

2. If so, what materials did you send to clients?

_____

_____

_____

_____

3. Where did you get the list of potential clients?

_____

_____

_____

_____

4. Who designed the mailing material (e.g., brochure or flyer)?

_____

_____

_____

5. Who actually did the mailing?

_____

_____

_____

_____

6. How frequently has your business used direct mailings?

_____

_____

_____

_____

ADVERTISING

1. If your business has paid for advertising, what media did you use?
   - ❏ Daily newspaper distributed city-wide
   - ❏ Weekly newspaper distributed city-wide
   - ❏ Daily newspaper distributed to a limited audience (e.g., a university paper)
   - ❏ Weekly newspaper distributed to a limited audience (e.g., an entertainment weekly)
   - ❏ Trade, professional, or organization publication
   - ❏ Popular magazine
   - ❏ Radio
   - ❏ Television
   - ❏ Yellow Pages

2. What were you usually promoting in these ads?
   - ❏ A special event (e.g., sales, grand opening)
   - ❏ An individual service
   - ❏ A general awareness of your firm
   - ❏ Other (specify): _____

3. Generally, what were the costs of your ads in the different media?

Advertisement	Medium	Cost	Ad size

4. Who designed or produced your ads?

_____

_____

_____

5. In your judgment, was the appearance of the ads professional?

_____

_____

6. Did you repeat the ads or run them once?

❑ Ran ads once   ❑ Repeated ads

7. Why did you choose this type of advertising schedule?

_____

_____

_____

8. Were the ads effective?

_____

_____

_____

INTERNET

1. Have you developed a Web site to promote your service to your clients?
   ❏ Yes   ❏ No
   Explain: _____

   _____

2. Who designed or produced your Web site?

   _____

   _____

3. How often do you update the site?
   ❏ Weekly   ❏ Monthly   ❏ When necessary
   Explain: _____

4. Do you use the site to promote your service or to actively sell? Explain:

   _____

   _____

   _____

5. How do you monitor "hits" on your site and receive feedback?

   _____

   _____

6. How effective has your Internet presence been to your business?

   _____

   _____

   _____

TELEMARKETING

1. Have you used the telephone to actively market or solicit clients?

   ❏ Yes   ❏ No

2. If not, why not? _____

   _____

   _____

3. If so, what is your primary reason for using the telephone as a sales tool?

   ❏ Qualify potential clients

   ❏ Set up appointments

   ❏ Sell over the phone

   ❏ Follow up calls

   ❏ Service existing and previous clients

   ❏ Other (specify): _____

4. How often do you use the telephone for marketing?

   ❏ 10 – 20% of the time

   ❏ 20 – 35% of the time

   ❏ 35 – 50% of the time

   ❏ Over 50% of the time

5. What creates the most obstacles for you in using the telephone to sell?

   ❏ Getting to the right person

   ❏ Introducing your business to new prospective clients

   ❏ Dealing with resistance (e.g., "We are happy with our current service.")

   ❏ Selling to someone you can't see

   ❏ Closing an appointment

   ❏ Other (specify): _____

6. What distractions (e.g., physical, mental, or environmental) do you encounter when using the telephone?

_____

_____

7. What areas of telemarketing (e.g., opening, presentation, and closing) or skills (e.g., probing, listening, and closing) need strengthening?

_____

_____

_____

PROMOTION SUMMARY

Summarize the information developed about your business's promotion. (Use other pages if necessary.) Remember to include both general and specific information about each promotion technique:

- Direct sales
- Public speaking
- Participating in organizations
- Direct mail
- Internet

- Publicity
- Referrals
- Sales promotion
- Advertising
- Telemarketing

_____

_____

_____

_____

_____

_____

_____

_____

_____

_____

WORKSHEET #6
CLIENT CHARACTERISTICS

Client (business or individual)	Duration (how long has client done business with you?)	Average sales ($)	When did client buy your service (e.g., season, month)?	How did client learn about your service (e.g., by referral, ads)?

INDIVIDUAL CLIENTS

1. What is the average age of your clients?

   ❑ 25 and under   ❑ 41 – 50

   ❑ 26 – 30   ❑ 51 – 60

   ❑ 31 – 35   ❑ Over 60

   ❑ 36 – 40

2. What percentage of your clients are male/female?

   ___ % Female _____ % Male

3. Where do your clients reside? (Use postal codes or street addresses to determine this information, if necessary.)

   _____

   _____

   _____

4. What is your clients' average annual household income?

   ❑ $20,000 and under

   ❑ 20,000 – 24,999

   ❑ 25,000 – 29,999

   ❑ 30,000 – 39,999

   ❑ 40,000 – 49,999

   ❑ 50,000 and over

5. What is the primary reason your clients use your service?

   _____

   _____

   _____

   _____

BUSINESS CLIENTS

1. Assess the size of your clients' businesses (based on number of employees and assets) and years in business:

Client   Size   Years

_____

_____

_____

_____

_____

_____

_____

_____

_____

2. Where are your clients located geographically?

_____

_____

_____

3. Can you estimate their annual gross sales?

❑ $29,000 and under   ❑ $100,000 – 149,999
❑   30,000 – 39,999   ❑   150,000 – 499,999
❑   40,000 – 49,999   ❑   500,000 – 1 million
❑   50,000 – 59,999   ❑   1 – 2 million
❑   60,000 – 69,999   ❑   2 – 3 million
❑   70,000 – 79,999   ❑   3 – 4 million
❑   80,000 – 89,999   ❑   4 – 5 million
❑   90,000 – 99,999   ❑   5 million and over

CLIENT CHARACTERISTICS SUMMARY

Summarize the five most common characteristics of your current clients:

1. _____

_____

_____

_____

_____

2. _____

_____

_____

_____

_____

3. _____

_____

_____

_____

_____

4. _____

_____

_____

_____

_____

5. _____

_____

_____

_____

_____

WORKSHEET #7
COMMUNICATIONS AND SERVICE

CUSTOMER AND CLIENT COMMUNICATIONS

1. Consider your company brochure, letterhead, and business cards. What image do these public relations items communicate to your clients?

   _____

   _____

   _____

2. Are the letters sent from your office accurately typed or do they contain typographical errors? _____

   _____

   _____

3. How do you (and your staff, if appropriate) answer your office phone?

   Do you answer promptly? _____

   What is the quality of your voice (e.g., pleasant, abrupt)? _____

   Do you speak rapidly or slowly so that you can be easily understood? _____

   Do you mumble, or do you speak distinctly? _____

4. Is your phone always answered during business hours (e.g., by a receptionist, office assistant, answering service, voice mail, or answering machine)?

   _____

   _____

   _____

5. Generally, how long does it take for you to return business calls?

   _____

   _____

   _____

6. If a problem occurs between your company and the client, how is it handled? (For example, do you contact the client as soon as possible? Do you meet the client personally or phone him or her?)

_____

_____

_____

_____

7. Is there a single aspect of your business that seems especially problematic? (For example, are your quotes frequently misunderstood? Must you often correct billings?)

_____

_____

_____

_____

8. Look around you. If clients come into your office, what image does your premises give them (e.g., businesslike or cluttered, organized or disorganized, in or out of control, barely surviving financially)?

_____

_____

_____

_____

9. How long are clients kept waiting when they come into your office?

_____

_____

_____

_____

CUSTOMER SERVICE

1. Do you send proposals or other client information when promised or requested by your clients?_____

   _____

   _____

2. Do you deliver the service your clients purchase?

   _____

   _____

   _____

3. Summarize the five most common characteristics of your current customers:

   1. _____

      _____

      _____

   2. _____

      _____

      _____

   3. _____

      _____

      _____

   4. _____

      _____

      _____

   5. _____

      _____

      _____

CLIENT INFORMATION SUMMARY

Summarize in narrative form what you've learned about your clients and your communications with and services to them.

_____
_____
_____
_____
_____
_____
_____
_____
_____
_____
_____
_____
_____
_____
_____
_____
_____
_____
_____
_____
_____
_____
_____
_____
_____
_____
_____
_____

WORKSHEET #8
SALES ANALYSIS

GENERAL SALES ANALYSIS

1. What is the dollar value of sales during the last 12-month period? $ _____

2. What percentage increase or decrease was this over the previous 12-month period?

   _____

3. How many clients did your firm service? _____

4. What was the average size of sales? (Divide total dollar value of sales by number of clients.) _____

5. How much did it cost your firm to make these sales?

Cost of salaries	$_____	
Overhead (rent, utilities)	$_____	
Other costs	$_____	
Total	$_____	$_____

6. Subtract costs from sales to determine your annual net profit. $ _____

7. Is there a predictable trend to your sales? For example, are sales of your service seasonal, cyclical, or irregular?

   _____

   _____

   _____

8. What do you consider to be the dollar value of a large, medium, and small sale?

   Large sale _____

   Medium sale _____

   Small sale _____

CLIENT SALES ANALYSIS

1. How many new clients purchased your service in the last 12 months?

   _____

   _____

2. What percentage increase of new clients was this over the previous 12 months?
   _____%

3. What size purchase did each client make in the last 12 months?
   Large sale   Medium sale   Small sale

   _____

   _____

   _____

   _____

   _____

   _____

   _____

4. How frequently do these clients, especially those in the "large sale" category, use your service?

   _____

   _____

   _____

   _____

   _____

   _____

   _____

   _____

5. Can you identify any common classes of these clients? (For example, do women age 35 to 40 tend to use your service often? Do professionals, such as architects and engineers, consistently make medium-sized purchases of your service?)

_____

_____

_____

_____

_____

_____

_____

GEOGRAPHICAL SALES ANALYSIS

1. Where were most of your sales made during the last 12-month period (e.g., from which office or outlet)?

_____

_____

_____

2. What size sale was made in each place?

Large sales _____

_____

_____

Medium sales _____

_____

_____

Small sales _____

_____

_____

SERVICE SALES ANALYSIS

1. How much sales revenue did each service make for your firm during the last 12-month period?

Service   Sales (in $)

_____

_____

_____

_____

2. Rank these services from "highest selling" (#1) to "lowest selling."

_____

_____

_____

_____

SALES ANALYSIS SUMMARY

Summarize here the information you developed in the sales report. Remember to include all four aspects of your analysis.

- General sales information
- Sales by geographical area
- Sales by client
- Sales by service

_____

_____

_____

_____

_____

_____

_____

THE FIFTH P

a. THE FIFTH P: PEOPLE

Before you step outside your firm and begin your analysis of its four P's, consider one more P: your people. Employees and partners comprise this fifth P, which is usually overlooked in traditional marketing. Yet, the people working in the firm are essential to every service business, for it is those people who deliver the service that can make the difference between a firm barely surviving or genuinely thriving.

Many studies conducted with customers of small and large service businesses confirm that customers' impressions of the firm are communicated by employees — particularly by people on the front lines. Research confirms this: whether customers originally decide to buy services from firms or whether they have concerns or complaints later about the quality of the service or its delivery.

A customer or client who feels positive about your service may tell up to five people about the value of your business and the service you deliver. If, however, a customer's impression or experience with your business is negative, he or she may tell as many as 15 to 19 people about the experience.

All clients have expectations about what will happen when they hire a firm to provide services. The firm's marketing communicates a promise to them — one that must be matched by their experience. The people who work for you *must* ensure that expectations are matched (and perhaps even exceeded!) so that clients walk away feeling successful and happy with your services.

Your employees can be indispensable in helping make decisions about how to best market to your clients. You look at your business through one set of eyeglasses labeled "owner" or "manager," and you can use customer surveys and other feedback mechanisms in this book as a second set of eyeglasses called "client." But you can discover a third set of eyeglasses to look at your business through the eyes of your employees or partners — particularly employees who work on the front lines who have accumulated useful insights about your service, your location, your prices, your promotion, and the way customers respond to company policies. The secrets of your front line may be an invaluable pool of wisdom you can dip into as you develop marketing strategies.

This practice has dual benefits. First, you obviously create a more viable marketing plan. Second, involving your employees helps them savor the importance of their jobs and their impact on the bottom line.

A small architectural firm involved its employees in developing its marketing plan — including the receptionist who had not been previously involved in marketing discussions and, therefore, had little "ownership" in the firm's marketing activities. The principal asked the receptionist for feedback from her perspective of dealing with customers calling or visiting the office. She was also asked to contribute ideas for strategies that would improve client service. She made suggestions of such material importance that they changed the way the firm interacted with its clients. Afterward, she felt a particular importance in how her role helped the firm be successful, and she demonstrated this at work daily.

b. THE FUTURE AND THE FIFTH P

Demographers tell us that the number of younger people in the workforce is shrinking. If your firm requires younger people to be able to deliver its services, or if it needs highly skilled people, be forewarned that a key business resource, the workforce, is slowly stabilizing, if not shrinking.

This shift in our workforce can result in excellent workers finding good jobs in all kinds of corporations. When larger organizations can offer an assortment of benefits as inducement to retaining good workers, smaller firms find it much more challenging to keep qualified personnel.

Did you know that any job today may be altogether different five years from now? Recognizing this, major corporations are focusing on training their people and creating opportunities that will spawn competitive workers in the 21st century. A small business can find itself caught between the shorter-term (and essential) goal of operating a profitable enterprise while still responding to another long-term necessity: keeping its workforce finely honed so that the business remains profitable in the future.

c. ANALYZING YOUR PEOPLE

To measure the marketing effectiveness of the people in your business, first analyze individual strengths and weaknesses of those you employ in terms of how you think clients might respond to them in delivering services. You may be able to draw some of this information from your company's performance appraisals. However, don't be surprised if, like many firms, you may not have been viewing employees in terms of client service and marketing. Worksheet #9 will help guide you and your employees.

Also, ask your individual employees to assess themselves. What do they perceive as their strengths and weaknesses? what else do they need to do to improve in marketing and/or client service? Ultimately, strive for a document that can be used mutually as a tool to discuss the differences between your perceptions.

In addition, analyze what marketing skills your people may lend to the firm. Do this with a dedication to actually using these skills. Some firms we have worked with have had skilled employees who enjoyed editing, writing, and creative work, but who had not written any promotional material. Such employees may assist you by writing your firm's newsletter, drafting its publicity releases, or helping you write articles to submit to a journal or newspaper.

You may also have employees who like organizing events. They can be particularly helpful planning an open house or some other client function. If you are uncertain about your employees' skills or interests, ask them to fill out Worksheet #10.

d. ANALYZING THE PROCESS

Do not stop with an employee analysis. Be bold enough to look at what might be happening in employee's jobs every day to keep them from being effective in the delivery of excellent customer service and in selling to new clients. One mechanism for achieving this is to do a functional job analysis.

Have people identify, step by step, the process involved to do their jobs. Or, bring a focus group of employees together to analyze the procedures used. Once it is clear how work is done, work together to make tasks simpler and more efficient. By doing so, you may enable your people to focus more on customers and less on procedures and paper.

A very small community bank wanted their customer service representatives to emphasize customers over paperwork. Because no analysis of the workload and the work flow had ever been done, each time a representative spent more time assisting a customer and making sales, his or her paperwork (and the backlog) increased tremendously. By the end of the day, when customers walked through the doors, sales representatives avoided serving them. After an analysis of the procedures and expectations of the job, management helped them streamline their work so that it really became a reward to work with customers — not a punishment.

e. MAKING THE CHANGES

Your analysis of people and processes may lead you to understand changes that must occur to support the firm's marketing efforts. You may determine that better communications between the employees or partners in your firm will be needed to effectively market your services. You may decide that you need to hold more effective meetings to communicate marketing activities and their results. It may also become clear that additional training will be needed to help your people recognize and seize opportunities to more effectively sell your service to clients.

A number of resources are available to you, ranging from courses taught in community colleges, mini-courses taught at chambers of commerce, half-day courses taught by national training organizations that send instructors to your area, and one-on-one coaching and training that can be delivered by private consultants and trainers. Depending on the needs and/or the resources available, you may want to consider sending your employees to a training session or bring someone in to customize training specific to your business and your needs. If you do, remember that effective training results in changing behavior, not just giving people more information.

Carefully identify how far the gap is between where you would like your employees to be and where they are at the moment. Assess whether a one-day workshop will be enough or whether they may need some ongoing training.

In addition to more formalized training, consider on-the-job and in-house training you may deliver to your employees. This training could help ensure that they follow the procedures or implement the approaches you have developed for your firm.

f. THE MOST IMPORTANT P

In summary, regardless of how you analyze your staff, it is acutely important that today — and into the next century — the human resource component of your business will either enhance your ability to be successful or detract from it. The investment you make will pay off many times if you recognize that through your people comes the special flavor and color of your firm and the many dimensions of your ability to be successful.

WORKSHEET #9
ASSESSING INDIVIDUAL STRENGTHS AND WEAKNESSES

Name:	Strengths	Weaknesses
1. Overall:		
2. Working with clients:		
3. Marketing and promotional skills:		

WORKSHEET #10
EMPLOYEES' SKILLS AND INTERESTS

1. Skills: Areas of some proficiency (work or general) (e.g., organizing, writing)

_____

_____

_____

_____

_____

_____

_____

_____

_____

2. Interests: Areas of interest, not necessarily proficient (e.g., learning about publicity, working with media, interested in systems, office, and other)

_____

_____

_____

_____

_____

_____

_____

_____

_____

_____

_____

_____

7
GATHERING THE FACTS ABOUT OUTSIDE INFLUENCES

a. ADDRESSING THE BUSINESS ENVIRONMENT

Spending your energy analyzing your own service business or professional practice may prove very satisfying. When you discover something wrong inside your firm, you can easily repair it. However, to thoroughly understand your service business is to understand only a tiny piece of the business puzzle. You must also understand the outside factors to which your service business is vulnerable.

Despite the importance of these larger pieces in the business puzzle, most service providers only infrequently consider them. "How can I predict what interest rates will be doing later this year?" the owner of an auto repair shop can reasonably ask. "Economists can't even agree! And who knows if my parts supplier will go on strike?" Similarly, the managing partner in a law firm could resist considering the firm's competition because the clientele has been stable for years, and the lawyer expects it to remain stable.

It is disturbing to address outside factors like competition, industry trends, inflation and interest rates, and technical innovation simply because they are outside your control. Many of us went into business for ourselves to "do it my way" — never realizing that many business influences would be out of our control much of the time.

If you know the outside influences, though, you know all the possibilities you may face. You need to understand the competition to position your business effectively. You need to consider interest rates, industry trends, and growth rates to plan for the future.

b. ANALYZING THE COMPETITION

Service providers may or may not believe it is necessary to know the competition. It is easy to ignore competitors because they, like most service businesses, tend to be smaller and less easy to identify and analyze. Yet, when a competitor is clearly understood, the more flexible nature of a service business allows subtle changes that can dramatically improve a company's competitive position.

To analyze your competitors, you must first identify them. Both factual information and subjective judgment are needed. Factual information includes the following:

- Who are the firms that compete?

61

- What services do they sell?
- How do they provide their services and, if significant, where do they provide them?
- How do they promote their service to potential clients?
- Who are their clients?

Subjective information about your competition includes your own perception, as well as that of your associates, of their competitive position, such as the advantages and disadvantages they have in the marketplace.

Much of this information is surprisingly available. Following are some ways to find it:

- Make your first list of competitors from the Yellow Pages in cities where your company markets its services.
- Order brochures from competitors. If some of your competitors are large enough to be public companies, request their annual reports. Study what competitors say about themselves.
- Once you have brochures and annual reports, you'll have Web site addresses for your competitors. Check out their Internet presence. How sophisticated is it? What do they offer on the Internet?
- Libraries frequently clip articles about local companies. Ask in the business section for newspaper or magazine articles about your competitors.
- While you're in the library, ask for directories in your profession. Some may have information you'd find helpful.

- Ask the librarian for trade association information and relevant studies.
- You can learn a great deal about your competitors at meetings of your professional association.
- Ask well-informed, businesslike colleagues you might consider "information brokers." Your brokers should know your service, your industry, and a lot of other businesspeople.
- Hire someone to call competitors for you. Give the caller, who should be an individual with presence and poise, a list of information you want to know. You may choose to have your caller say that he or she is doing a student project, looking for a job, or considering a career change.
- Use your competitors' services. For example, a hair stylist might have his or her hair cut in a competitor's shop.
- Run a want ad presenting yourself as a buyer of services and requesting proposals from competitors.

Your research methods will depend on your personal and professional ethics. Whichever methods you choose, however, you'll need to be able to complete two types of analyses — one factual, the other subjective. Collecting the factual information requires more effort, and the subjective analysis requires more thought. For example, a great deal of critical evaluation is needed to identify the advantages and disadvantages of a small engineering firm compared to a large firm. The advantages might be —

- more personalized contact with clients,
- more frequent client contact with key partners,

- ability to tailor services and dates to the client, and

- established, cohesive teamwork among employees.

The disadvantages might be —

- a limited depth of expertise among the engineers,

- more demand on key partners, who may be spread too thin between clients and administrative demands,

- a possible lack of resources (e.g., people, money, or equipment) to bring to the client, and

- a higher cost.

Use Worksheet #11 to record the facts about your competition and Worksheet #12 to compare the competition to your company.

c. POSITIONING: THE PURPOSE OF COMPETITIVE ANALYSIS

Knowing your competition well has a singular purpose: to make your service business or professional practice more competitive. In sales interviews with prospective clients, you'll be better able to describe how you can be of service. Your business will be even more successful if you take an aggressive stance, determine in advance what your differences are, and describe it consistently to your clients.

Identifying how your business is different from its competition is what marketers call *positioning*. Positioning assumes that your prospective clients don't, won't, or can't tell the differences between your firm and others most of the time. Thus, you must tell them how your service differs. You can do this through a positioning statement.

For example, if your business provides speech and presentations training services to individuals, through positioning you might describe your services like this:

Teaching individuals to use their voices and body language to speak more effectively and persuasively; to prepare and deliver clear, effective presentations; to overcome anxiety; and to create a powerful, positive presence.

Use Worksheet #13 to write your position statement. (See chapter 9 for more on positioning after you have identified your target markets.)

d. LOOKING AHEAD IN GENERAL

Part of looking ahead as a service provider is asking a simple but compelling question: What is happening that will affect my service business in the next year? From the information you collect in answer to this question, you can make assumptions that will help you anticipate the short-term future. The question should be asked about the following outside influences:

- the status of the local or national economy,

- a threatened strike in a related industry,

- the inflation rate

- the status of major competitors,

- the economic well-being of a major industry or your client in that industry, and

- a major technical innovation that may be either expected or unexpected.

Not all factors are relevant to every business. Which are important to your firm?

WORKSHEET #11
THE COMPETITION

Identification of competitor	Description of competition				
	Service	Price	Place	Promotion	Clients

Competitor	Competitor advantages	Competitor disadvantages

WORKSHEET #12
YOUR COMPANY AND THE COMPETITION

1. Now that you've analyzed the competition, determine what the major differences are between your service business and your competition. (For example, do you deliver your service in a different way? Is your company smaller or larger than that of your competitors?) _____

   _____

   _____

   _____

2. Do several of these differences fall into similar categories?
   ❏ Service differences
   ❏ Client differences
   ❏ Other (specify): _____
   ❏ No similarities in categories

3. What are your company's advantages and disadvantages?
   Service differences

List individual differences (from #1)	How does this difference give you an advantage over the competition?	How is this difference a disadvantage to your company?

   Client differences

List individual differences (from #1)	How does this difference give you an advantage over the competition?	How is this difference a disadvantage to your company?

Once you've determined which factors are important, you will want to find out more about them.

Information about the short-term future is available to service providers through both formal and information sources. Information may be collected now for your marketing plan, but to be of greatest value to your service business or professional practice it should be sought continually.

Publications are the primary or formal sources of such information. These include the *Wall Street Journal, Business Week, Inc.,* trade publications, weekly and monthly local business magazines, and local newspapers. Economic broadcasts, which often summarize such information, may save time and provide the overview needed to answer the question.

Also use secondary or informal sources. Individuals who track business trends can prove invaluable; simply ask them for help. If using the services of others without compensation feels unethical to you, pay for the information or barter something that is important to them. Money, services, or information that makes their jobs easier are all worthwhile methods of compensation.

Use Worksheet #14 to record the information you find.

e. THE NATURE OF ASSUMPTIONS

Having asked and come to conclusions about the factors that affect your business, rewrite your conclusions, or assumptions, in a way that captures their essence. For service providers who prefer to deal in facts or figures, assumptions by their very nature may prove particularly difficult for the following reasons:

- Assumptions are unprovable. Usually, they are based on uncertain evidence.

- Assumptions are forward looking. They anticipate the future, usually the coming year.

- Assumptions are information based. They are usually the conclusions you come to as a result of collecting information.

- Assumptions are broad and narrow. Some are about broad factors, such as the economy. Others are about narrow factors, such as your expectations about your company.

- Assumptions are controllable and uncontrollable. They are made about controllable factors, such as your company's capabilities. Others are made about uncontrollable factors, such as the local economy or a competitor's new product.

For example, you might conclude from your formal and informal sources that the economy will slide into a recession during the next year. As a result, your assumption might be, "Tight money will make it harder to get a loan for our planned expansion into the new market."

Use Worksheet #15 to record your assumptions.

f. LOOKING AHEAD THROUGH INDUSTRY TRENDS

Looking ahead at the specific industry of which your service business or professional practice is a part is also important. To determine which trends are significant

WORKSHEET #13
POSITION STATEMENT

1. Identify the type of service your business provides.

   _____

   _____

   _____

2. Specify how your business is different from your competitors in the service you provide, your fee structure, the way you provide service, the way you promote your service, and your clients.

   _____

   _____

   _____

3. Now, write about that difference in a concise, jargon-free statement.

   _____

   _____

   _____

   _____

   _____

   _____

   _____

   _____

   _____

   _____

   _____

   _____

   _____

   _____

POSITION STATEMENT SUMMARY

Summarize the kind of competition you face and your position in response to it.

_____

_____

_____

_____

_____

_____

_____

_____

_____

_____

_____

_____

_____

_____

_____

_____

_____

_____

_____

_____

_____

_____

_____

_____

WORKSHEET #14
OUTSIDE INFLUENCES IMPORTANT TO YOUR SERVICE

Outside influence	Important to business?		Reason
	Yes	No	
Status of local economy:			
Status of national economy:			
Rate of inflation:			
Labor relations in _____ industry:			
Economic well-being of _____ (key client, industry):			
Status of _____ (major competitor):			
Status of _____ (major innovation):			

to you, explore the marketing elements of your industry. These include the following:

- General changes in the industry
- Changes in services in your field
- Pricing changes
- Changes in the way your service is distributed or delivered to clients
- Possible changes in promotion
- Changes in the clients themselves

Some examples of these changes are —

- *General industry change:* A consulting firm might note that reduced government budgets will result in staff layoffs and potentially greater use of consultants.
- *Service change:* A training firm might surmise that greater acceptance of training with video or audio tapes, rather than through classroom instruction, may reduce the need for teachers.
- *Pricing change:* An accounting firm may find that clients' expectations for set project or retainer fees force the firm to be more efficient and client-oriented.
- *Service distribution change:* A hair salon might refuse to continue offering manicures, given what its owner considers a punitive commission schedule required by manicurists. The owner may prefer to set up a joint venture or mutual referrals with a nail salon.
- *Promotion change:* A medical clinic may find it needs to provide patients with more communication and personal contact to retain their loyalty and receive referrals from them.
- *Change in clients:* A law firm may see a shift from large corporate clients to a more diverse small business clientele.

The best formal source of information about industry trends is your professional or trade associations' publications. If you don't receive magazines and newsletters from your associations, your public or university library may have them.

The chief informal source of information is your participation in the organizations themselves and your discussions with knowledgeable professionals in your field.

The kind of information you draw from your sources will depend on your business. For example, a landscape architect might research topics as diverse as emerging design concepts, new methods of managing client relationships within the profession, or land use changes as more multiple, rather than single unit, dwellings are built.

Use Worksheet #16 to consolidate the information you gather about industry trends.

WORKSHEET #15
ASSUMPTIONS ABOUT THE FUTURE

Factors that might affect your service business in the next year	How might each factor affect your business?
Sample: *Recession*	Tight money will make it harder to get a loan and expand business.

ASSUMPTIONS SUMMARY

Summarize assumptions about next year's operations.

_____
_____
_____
_____
_____
_____
_____
_____
_____
_____
_____
_____
_____
_____
_____
_____
_____
_____
_____
_____
_____
_____
_____

WORKSHEET #16
INDUSTRY TRENDS AND THEIR IMPACT

1. What coming changes in your industry may affect your service business?

_____

_____

_____

2. What future changes in services in your field may affect your service business?

_____

_____

_____

3. Are there anticipated future changes in fees that may affect your service business?

_____

_____

_____

4. What anticipated future distribution changes may affect your service business?

_____

_____

_____

5. What anticipated future promotion changes may affect your service business?

_____

_____

_____

6. What are the anticipated changes clients may make that might affect your service business?

_____

_____

INDUSTRY TRENDS SUMMARY

Summarize the industry trends you've identified.

_____

_____

_____

_____

_____

_____

_____

_____

_____

_____

_____

_____

_____

_____

_____

_____

_____

_____

_____

_____

_____

_____

_____

_____

_____

8

DISCOVERING PROBLEMS AND OPPORTUNITIES

a. INTEGRATION: THE NAME OF THE MARKETING GAME

Now that you have gathered information in an internal analysis of your firm and in an external analysis of economic influences, integrate the two sets of information. Use two categories — clarifying marketing problems and identifying marketing opportunities — to reduce your morass of internal and external information to its essentials.

b. SEEING PROBLEMS PROPERLY

Every business owner knows *what* problems are. In integrating your information, it is also helpful to know *how* to look at problems from a marketing perspective.

First, define the problems broadly as things that need correction. Here are some ways to identify problems:

- Is there a deviation from anticipated results? Fewer clients than you expected? A drop in awareness about your firm or its services?

- Is something preventing the smooth functioning of your firm's marketing effort? A lack of personnel? Inadequate promotional literature (such as the brochure that was never completed)?

- Do obstacles stand in the way of achieving a marketing goal? Are your salespeople unable to reach decision makers? Are clients dissatisfied with your service? Are the benefits of using your service unclear?

Second, consider problems that relate to marketing only. Those are problems in the following areas:

- The service your service business or private practice offers

- Personnel who deliver the service

- How your service is distributed or the place from which it is distributed

- Fee you charge for your service

- How you promote your service to prospective clients

- The clients themselves

- Sales made to those clients

If you are a typical service provider, you may find it easier to think of management and financial problems. You may be irritated that work is not getting done on time or to your standards because the staff seem to be wasting time or making errors. You may be frustrated if expenses are too high or worried if income is too low. But don't permit other business problems to intrude on preparing your marketing plan just because they seem more urgent or are more controllable than the unknown realm of marketing.

Third, ask yourself if what looks like a problem is *really* the problem, or just a symptom of one. Problems, including marketing problems, are often more complex than they seem. For example, consider the following problem: Sales of retail products aren't high enough in a hair salon. Frequently selected brands of shampoo or hair spray don't move. Is the problem that the hair designers aren't motivated to sell anything but services? Or are the low sales a symptom that the hair designers aren't trained to sell products? Or are the low sales a symptom that the products don't suit the target market?

Consider another example. In a law firm, the number of billable hours are lower than in the past. Is this a symptom of the needs of a changing clientele? Have key lawyers been lost to other firms? Are the lawyers with the best contacts doing too much administrative work? Is development of the practice a low priority in the firm?

It is essential to consider each problem dynamically, to look at how each changes in relation to the other. In evaluating the problems you identify, consider the following:

- If this is just a symptom, what is the real problem?
- Will solving the problem lead to favorable change in your current market position? For example, would developing clear expectations of staff regarding marketing produce desired results?
- Is this an industry problem or a company problem? For example, is the fact that engineers are reluctant to make sales calls something that most firms deal with, or is it a problem at just your firm?

Look beyond the obvious; be analytical. Objectively separate bias from information. Talk with your advisers, such as your accountant, with whom you have a formal relationship. Seek the advice of informal sources, such as a mentor, who will keep your confidence.

Finally, realize that some problems will be out of your control. A declining economy in which many lose their jobs will create hardships for professionals such as dentists. Families will delay getting checkups, cleanings, and fillings. Conversely, an out-of-control inflation rate and high interest rates might particularly affect such professionals as architects.

Knowing what uncontrollable factors *could* affect your business and how they might do so can help you make better decisions. For example, anticipating a potential recession could result in your modifying promotion plans and arriving at your marketing goals later. Expecting changes in personnel might influence you to look for recruits or revise your plans for entering a new market area.

c. CREATING OPPORTUNITIES

Just as every service provider knows what problems are, most can also tell what an opportunity is: an exploitable circumstance that can be turned into more sales, result in higher profit, or give the firm a competitive edge through marketing action. While many service providers can cite incidents when they *reacted* to a chance and took an opportunity for the firm, fewer are able to *create* such opportunities.

Would you, for example, be able to create an opportunity as did this parking lot owner in a major western city? When his city's employment rate was very high and few people could afford hourly parking, he created more business by washing the windshields of cars in his lots.

His success illustrates what is needed: an entrepreneur's vision and the ability to combine what is happening in the market with a special, different way the company can respond to it.

For example, your service might create an opportunity by supplying a systems solution to the complex problem of technological change, as did a computer consulting firm. This firm works with its clients throughout selection of hardware and software, identifying client needs, preparing specifications for vendors, receiving bids, advising clients in selection, overseeing installation of the system, adapting software as needed, and training staff to use it.

Changing technology might present an opportunity in other ways. For example, people are no longer educated for life, so opportunities abound for trainers in fields such as manufacturing (steel and automotive) and other high tech, labor-intensive industries. As well, the intellectual resources of specialists are needed in many professions now to guide firms through the thicket of increasing competition to find ways to apply new technology. For example, the latest, most sophisticated equipment that quickly repairs injured muscles might create a technological opportunity for a physical therapy practice.

Discovering your "market niche" means serving your clients in a way no one else is. A law firm that offers only mediation

services to divorcing clients is one example. Another is a small accounting firm providing part-time controller services to small firms that cannot afford full-time staff. A third is a travel agency offering seminars in travel planning, clothing, and accessories for working professionals.

Your firm may find a more effective way of selling or distributing its services. A training firm might invest in video training programs, for example, to increase both the number of people it can serve and its sales.

Your clients may be changing. Is there, for example, a way to serve the whole client, even though you are now qualified to provide only one part of a service? An accountant who is expert at historical financial analysis might enlist the services of a certified financial planner who knows investment opportunities.

Can you take advantage of your location? Are businesses that use your service clustered in one geographical area? Or if you're like many services — less focused on a specific area — can you take advantage of a geographical bias? For example, do legal clients in your area believe that the really good law firms are located in big buildings downtown rather than in the suburbs?

Can you create additional opportunities by using your financial strength, as did a market research firm that expanded its unique approach to a second and then a third city?

d. SEEING THROUGH PROBLEMS TO OPPORTUNITIES

You make money not by focusing on problems, but by solving them. Among the biggest challenges a service provider faces is looking past daily problems and seeing the possibilities beyond. Here are some ways to see opportunities where you now see only problems.

Ask questions that help you see the possible rather than the impossible:

Don't say: We tried that before.
Ask: What has changed since we tried it?

Don't say: It costs too much.
Ask: Can we make a profit from it? How much will it save the company?

Don't say: It won't work.
Ask: Which part will work?

Don't say: It's too radical a change.
Ask: What progress can be attained from the change?

Don't say: I don't have the time.
Ask: What can be deleted?

Don't say: We've never done it that way before.
Ask: What change is needed so we can do it the new way?

Thoughts can create reality. Your thought that a problem is impossible to overcome will erect seemingly impossible barriers. Your thought that it must be possible may lead to solutions.

Realize that many opportunities arise out of problems. Think of a problem as being the tails side of a coin. When you flip it, you will find the opportunities that grow out of the problem on the heads side.

Treat the problem as neutral. Call it a *situation* rather than the more emotionally loaded *problem.* Then, evaluate the type of situation.

- Is it an *environmental* situation, such as where your office is located?

- Is it a *group* situation, such as a secretary who is shared with other professionals and does not send out your marketing materials?

- Is it an *individual* situation, such as three partners who want to sell, while another will not?

After consciously evaluating your problems, relegate them impartially to your subconscious. At times when your body is busy but your mind isn't — while driving, jogging, or showering — your mind will be working to solve your problems.

Use Worksheet #17 to look at your problems and opportunities.

WORKSHEET #17
PROBLEMS AND OPPORTUNITIES

CLASSIFICATION OF SITUATIONS			
Situations (good or bad) that may affect your business	Environmental (e.g., lighting in your shop, impending recession)	Group issue among personnel in your company	Individual issue (e.g., a problem of a single person in your company)

PROBLEM DYNAMICS				
Situations you define as problems	Is this really the problem, or is it a symptom of another problem?	Is it an industry or company problem?	Can you change this problem?	Can you control this problem?

PROBLEMS TO OPPORTUNITIES

1. Which of the situations would you identify as opportunities?

   _____

   _____

   _____

2. Think particularly of clients you might be selling to. What "market opportunities," as they are called, can you identify?

   _____

   _____

   _____

3. Review the problems you identified. List the problems on the tails side of the "coins" below. Mentally flip the problems over to the heads side of the coin to determine how they can be made into opportunities.

Example:

TAILS:
Small
firm

Flip

HEADS:
Can offer
owner's
attention to
each client

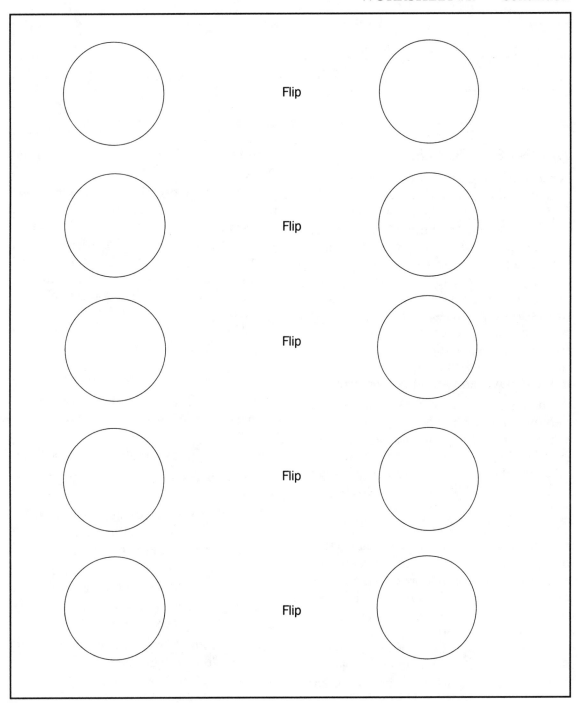

SETTING GOALS AND OBJECTIVES 9

a. WHY SET GOALS?

After marketing problems are recognized and marketing opportunities are identified, most people are then — and only then — able to decide what they want to achieve. Setting marketing goals is simply the process of laying the pathway to the future. Almost inevitably (given the nature of those who start service businesses or professional practices), service providers want to order that pathway, to construct from many possibilities their vision of the firm's future. To do so, in fact, is essential to the survival and growth of the firm.

The discipline of psychology has amply demonstrated the power of goals for individuals. When set, goals clarify and direct people. When achieved, goals provide a measure of success and inspire confidence in the future. Without goals, people lose interest in life.

Businesses, as the creation of people, *must* have a focus. This is particularly true of service businesses, which operate more at the preference of their owners than other types of businesses. Because a service business is, in some cases, literally and figuratively the person who formed it, marketing goals take on a special significance. When the service provider and the business are one, the firm's goals must be congruent with the life and professional goals of the person.

You must be prepared to live with your goals when you achieve them. The owner of a graphic design firm decided to hire a marketing person to increase the firm's business. However, as the marketing person successfully promoted the firm, the owner found that he had too much work and too few staff to do it. He was not prepared to make the changes necessary to live with the achievement of his goals.

b. WHAT ARE GOALS, ANYWAY?

Simply stated, goals are the long-term results you want your service business or professional practice to achieve.

In writing goals, remember the following:

- Goals are broad, sweeping statements.

- Goals are both realistic (so they can be achieved) and challenging (so you must strive to achieve them).

- Goals may be set for your personal or professional life and for your firm in general, or for each element in the marketing mix.

- Goals may overlap; therefore, they should be integrated.

c. CLARIFYING GOALS

As mentioned, the service provider lives a dual role as both an individual and a business owner. Thus, clarity about personal and professional goals is an essential foundation to marketing goals. For example, these are the life and professional goals of one service provider:

- *A general life goal:* To balance all parts of my life: career, family, and friends.
- *A general professional goal:* To have my colleagues acknowledge me as an expert in my field.

The company and marketing goals of the firm might be dramatically influenced by the service provider's personal goals:

- *A general company goal:* To be earning a net profit of $xxx annually by 2001. (That net profit will be affected by the service provider's wish to spend time pursuing other aspects of life that provide balance.)
- *A general marketing goal:* To establish and secure the west coast as our primary market. (Instead of, perhaps, choosing a national market or national prominence because of previous commitments.)

d. YOUR PERSONAL AND COMPANY GOALS

Once you understand the importance of knowing your own goals, it is essential that you clarify them and state them specifically. Let the following guide you as you set your goals:

- *Be honest with yourself.* Ultimately, your own wishes, not those of others, will dictate what you achieve. Future achievements will come most

comfortably if based on honest assumptions now.

- *Be passionate about these goals.* Passion is a word applied too infrequently in business. And in the clear, cool logic of developing any business plan, passion may seem inappropriate. But if you don't care deeply, the drive to achieve goals will be missing.

- *Be realistic about what's genuinely possible.* This is important when integrating diverse business goals. For example, a goal of increasing billable hours significantly and not increasing the number of staff to support those who work with clients may not be possible.

  Maturity becomes most important when integrating business goals with personal choices. For some service providers, total dedication to a business can provide professional recognition and financial rewards that almost eliminate the need for personal involvement. Others may feel the price of such dedication — to family, interests, even one's humanity — would be inordinately high. If you're in the latter group, you must adjust your sights.

- *Keep your perspective.* Goals are not irrevocably set. They can be changed, modified, or removed. They are a tool to use at will in business.

- *Visualize your goals.* Anticipate what success will look and feel like as a rehearsal for achieving goals. As you're setting each goal, ask yourself, "Can I see it?" If not, can you help yourself see it in time? Almost any service provider who has the discipline to succeed can certainly create the mental image that creates achievement.

Write down your personal and professional goals in Worksheet #18. Then use Worksheet #19 to record your firm's goals.

To set your company's goals, look five years into the future. What do you see? Where do you want to be? Write it down.

Think about the stepping stones along the way to that goal. What are the interim goals necessary to achieve that five-year goal? For example, if you want to be one of the top three accounting firms in the area in Year Five, what must you do in Years Four, Three, Two, and within the next year, Year One, to make it happen?

To achieve the five-year goal of being a leader in the accounting field, you would build the foundation as follows. Within the next year you would begin to focus on strengthening skills while minimizing weaknesses. Particularly, you would begin to build the kind of staff expertise needed in the firm you want to own.

In Year Two, you would encourage your associates to become involved in community and professional organizations where they would actively pursue speaking engagements and serve on committees. In Year Three, you would build community contacts (both one-on-one and through groups), as well as gain exposure through media. You and your associates would write articles and arrange interviews with reporters. Your account list would include significant accounts. In Year Four, you would reach out to other communities in your region. Members of your firm would continue to make speeches, write articles or books, and be involved with professional groups. By Year Five, your goal would be reached.

Expect that setting and integrating your own goals will require time and thought. It won't — and shouldn't — come easily.

e. MARKETING GOALS

From general company goals flow goals for financing, managing, and marketing your service business or professional practice. Having set general goals, service providers are presented with the challenge of spelling out more specific marketing goals. These might be anything that affect —

- the services a firm will offer or innovate,
- the fees charged,
- the place from which the business distributes its services or the way they are distributed,
- the way a professional practice intends to promote its service to people who might buy it,
- the clients the firm will provide those services to, and
- the amount of sales the firm will generate.

For example, if a general company goal is to make $250,000 in sales this year, the specific marketing goals might be the following:

- To sell 20% more of X service or Y service.
- To increase fees or marketable time by 10%.
- To improve client access to services over the telephone and through referral networks.

- To organize and systematize communication with potential and current clients and referrals.
- To focus more attention on existing clients by increasing opportunities to cross-sell.
- To increase overall sales by 25%.

f. SETTING YOUR COMPANY'S MARKETING GOALS FOR NEXT YEAR

Look again at your company's goals for the coming year. Sort out from the general goals any aspects that affect marketing. Now set your firm's specific marketing goals using Worksheet #20 as a guide.

g. SETTING OBJECTIVES

1. Why goals are never enough

Although goals are a guide for creating the future, they lack a certain immediacy that would help achieve them. Goals, which point you to the future, don't necessarily assure you will get there. Perhaps this is because doing the work that puts the goal in sight is more important — and more difficult.

In business, it is essential to communicate more than goals. You must specify *when* you will do *how much* of *what* to achieve the goal, that is, set objectives.

2. The role of objectives

Ideally, objectives generate the urgency that is needed to inspire you to achieve a goal. In practice, your objectives also present the best solution to problems identified in the firm. Objectives both inspire and provide solutions if they have the following three characteristics. An objective should be —

- specific and measurable,
- achieved within a limited time, and
- identified with an actual result.

Determining the result to be achieved sometimes creates confusion. Some service providers try to be too specific about how the objectives will be achieved when they should really be concerned with what will be achieved.

3. What does a typical objective look like?

Make your service available to more buyers. Fulfill more customer needs. Expand or change your service's distribution.

Build customer acceptance in a new market or for a new service. Increase total dollar sales per client. These are typical marketing objectives.

Objectives focus further attention on the following six marketing elements about which you have previously set goals:

- Services
- Fees
- Place or way service is distributed
- Promotion
- Clients to be served
- Sales

Whereas writing marketing goals is an exercise in vision, writing marketing objectives is an exercise in discipline. From the broadly drawn sketch of goals is rendered a detailed and precise portrait. Here are some examples of marketing objectives that are specific and time bound and that have a measurable end result.

(a) Service objectives

Introduce [*how many*] new services by [*specific date*].

Improve [*name of service*] by [*making which specific change*] before [*specific date*].

(b) Fee objectives

Raise fees [*amount*] on [*specific date*] so they are within [*percentage*] of similar services.

(c) Place objectives

Penetrate the [*city or defined region*] area more deeply by developing [*amount*] contracts by [*date*].

Move offices to a more appropriate [*amount*] square foot location in [*general area*] by [*date*].

(d) Promotion objectives

Increase awareness about the firm's services by [*how many*] colleagues before [*date*].

Develop a new brochure that outlines services more concisely by [*date*].

(e) Client objectives

Provide [*type*] services to [*how many*] [*specific type of clients*] by [*date*].

Have all professional staff producing [*how many*] billable hours of new client services by [*date*].

(f) Sales objectives

Sell [*definite amount*] by [*specific date*].

Increase the average order size to [*dollar value*] sales by [*date*].

h. INTEGRATING GOALS AND OBJECTIVES

To march forward into the future, you must set objectives that mesh with the goals you want to achieve. For example, a promotion goal of increasing the market's awareness of your firm's image must be integrated with promotion objectives that specify developing an effective brochure by the end of the year and selling 10% more services within six months.

Your task now is to integrate the marketing goal you want to achieve next year with the how much, what, and when required to achieve it.

Use Worksheet #21 to record the objectives that will lead you to the marketing goals set on Worksheet #20.

1. What is important to you — personally, professionally, and in your business?

_____

_____

_____

2. How much time does each aspect of life require of you?

_____

_____

_____

3. What are your lifetime business or professional goals?

_____

_____

_____

4. How would you like to spend the next three to five years in your business or profession?

_____

_____

_____

5. If you knew you would die six months from today, how would you spend your time until then?

_____

_____

_____

_____

_____

_____

WORKSHEET #19
COMPANY GOALS

Five-year goals:

_____

_____

_____

_____

Four-year goals:

_____

_____

_____

_____

Three-year goals:

_____

_____

_____

_____

Two-year goals:

_____

_____

_____

_____

Goals for next year, Year One:

_____

_____

_____

For services:

_____

_____

For fees:

_____

_____

_____

For place (the place from which you distribute your services or the way you distribute them):

_____

_____

_____

For the way the company is promoted:

_____

_____

_____

For clients:

_____

_____

_____

For the sales the company will generate:

_____

_____

_____

WORKSHEET #20 — Continued

GENERAL AND MARKETING GOALS SUMMARY

Summarize your company's general and marketing goals.

_____
_____
_____
_____
_____
_____
_____
_____
_____
_____
_____
_____
_____
_____
_____
_____
_____
_____
_____
_____
_____
_____
_____

1. Service goal:_____

   _____

   Service objective:_____

   _____

   _____

   Service objective:_____

   _____

   _____

2. Fee goal: _____

   _____

   Fee objective:_____

   _____

   _____

   Fee objective:_____

   _____

   _____

3. Place or way goal: _____

   _____

   Place or way objective: _____

   _____

   _____

   Place or way objective: _____

   _____

   _____

4. Promotion goal: _____

_____

Promotion objective: _____

_____

_____

Promotion objective: _____

_____

_____

5. Client goal: _____

_____

Client objective: _____

_____

_____

Client objective: _____

_____

_____

6. Sales goal: _____

_____

Sales objective: _____

_____

_____

Sales objective: _____

_____

_____

10
TARGET MARKETS AND POSITIONING

a. THE MARKETING MATCH

It's time now to make a series of careful selections that will aim your service business or professional practice toward achieving your marketing goals and objectives. Make your selection in three parts:

- Specify *who* your company's clients will be. In marketing terminology, these are called your *target markets*.

- Determine *what* your marketing appeal will be for them. As mentioned earlier, marketers call this *positioning*.

- Clarify *how* your firm will align its objectives, given your target markets and your market position. Marketers have a term for this, too. It's called hard work.

For clarity, the three who, what, and how selections are presented sequentially and in detail below. In reality, though, their selection occurs almost simultaneously, each evolving out of the other.

b. TARGETING YOUR MARKETS

Target markets can best be explained visually. Imagine every client who might use the type of service your firm offers, and consider that large group as 100% of a customer pie. For example, as an architect, you could serve individual home owners, developers of small commercial buildings, developers of skyscrapers, and government departments, each type of client representing one slice in the customer pie. Probably, though, you serve only one or two types of clients. You will not likely have the capacity or desire to serve every type of potential client. In target marketing you choose only a portion of the customer pie, say 3% of it. If your firm is larger, your percentage will be too. It increases as a small firm grows into a larger one.

Because your target markets are specific service users, you need to identify them as precisely as possible. Start by identifying five characteristics your clients have in common. Businesses serving individuals might consider the following:

- Demographics (e.g., age, sex, race, size of family, age of family, and number of adults in family, as well as where they live)

- Socioeconomic data (e.g., social class, occupation, level of education, and approximate annual income)

- Lifestyles (e.g., activities, interests, beliefs, and opinions)

- How frequently they use your kind of service (e.g., heavy, moderate, light, never)

Companies serving other businesses could consider the following:

- Demographic and financial data (e.g., type of industry, number of employees, annual sales volume, and geographical location)
- How they use your service (e.g., size of orders, buying volume, and seasonal buying patterns)

A couple of examples may help. A hair salon in an urban middle- to upper-class neighborhood serves professional women, among other target groups. These women have the following characteristics:

- They hold responsible jobs outside the home.
- They are 25 to 50 years old.
- Eighty percent are married; 20% are single.
- Most have children, the oldest of whom are teenagers.
- Most are members of families that have a combined income greater than $50,000.

Another company is a music distributor, providing customized, piped-in music to businesses. These businesses have the following characteristics:

- They work directly with the public.
- They usually have a lot of foot traffic.
- They believe the work atmosphere affects productivity.
- They make a profit (and so can consider additional expenditures).
- They may be small or large businesses.

The most successful target market descriptions emphasize demographics, the factors mentioned above. Demographics can be discovered easily, while less tangible characteristics (such as lifestyles, beliefs, and opinions) cannot. Demographics describe potential clients in the target market — not just their need for your firm's services.

Service businesses or professional practices can have more than one target market. For example, the hair salon mentioned has identified three: the professional women described above, traditional women, and younger professional men. The number of target markets your firm serves will depend on the size of your company as well as other factors. For example, a large law firm can provide more legal services to its clients than a smaller law firm.

In general, you'll want to specify enough markets so that your firm is not tied to only one industry. Otherwise, as that industry goes, so goes your firm. A printer with several computer customers learned this hard lesson when the computer industry suffered in the mid-1980s.

To help you expand into new markets, identify them as closely as you can. But characterizing a target market is difficult if you have not served it before. Research not only the demographics of the group you want to serve, but also whether they need or are interested in the service your firm offers.

Describe the members of your target market on Worksheet #22.

Accepting the concept of targeting is difficult for many service providers. Often, they fear losing business; other potential clients might contact them, they say. Or they might choose the wrong market, one that ultimately won't support the firm. Or they look around and see that the competition continues to take any client who walks through the door. In addition to business reasons for resisting limits on the market, there may be personal reasons. The service provider may be a generalist who fears constraints and boredom.

However, every business — even mammoth corporations — target their markets. Huge companies target by product line. Smaller businesses target to their slice of the customer pie. A specialty store featuring better women's clothing targets. A manufacturer of sophisticated scientific instrumentation targets. Both a deli that serves quick, healthy lunches to office workers and an elegant restaurant known for its romantic atmosphere target.

Service businesses must target their markets. Their owners recognize that it is better to serve those clients they can serve well than to randomly attempt to serve everyone and, given the complexity of specialities from medicine to car repair, serve them poorly.

The market also has a clearer image of what a business does when it targets. And the market trusts those service providers who are willing to say, "We do this very well. If you need something else done, we'll help you find the best person to assist you on that. And next time you need this done, we'll be here to help you." The market understands how complex professional disciplines are and looks to specialists who know their work thoroughly.

Yet, the fears about target markets remain. You may have some. To help you overcome your fears, test your markets, using Worksheet #23.

c. POSITIONING YOUR SERVICE

The two concepts — target markets and positioning — are symbiotic marketing principles. While target markets are the clients your firm will serve, positioning is the concerted, focused way you will present your service business or professional practice to them.

To claim a market position is to find a way of explaining the services your firm can provide to the target group you want to serve. Among the most successful position statements in American business was "We're Avis. We're Number 2. We try harder." Why? Because it separated one rental car company from others in the same business; because it made promises to its market of consumers; because it was believable; because it was simple, specific, concise — and memorable.

Car rental services (and virtually every other type of business) operate almost totally alike. To the public, they seem to be at least 80% alike 100% of the time. For example, a law firm can position itself and say, "Here is the way we differ 20% from our competitors: We specialize only in real estate law." A law firm might not want to overtly claim it's better than the others. But clearly stating what it does for which target markets separates that firm from the others. As discussed in chapter 7, knowing who your competitors are is essential in positioning your company. For example, given the abundance of general travel agencies, your agency might be wise to specialize in cruises. Likewise, a therapist in an urban area where many professional therapists practice might concentrate on relationship counseling or life's transitions. And a graphic design firm might become a sign specialist.

Each firm has identified a target market, then established a specialty and position for that market, at least in theory. In practice, it is more likely that the service provider lets his or her interests lead the way to a market position, forgetting the target market altogether. Typically, when this happens, the service provider learns positioning the hard way as the market educates the business on whether the arbitrary position is workable. Market research reduces the risk of claiming a market position no one wants.

If a service business serves different markets with several services, different market positions may be needed for each. Consider the example of a consulting firm that offers both health care and telecommunications consulting. In offering health care consultation to its health care providers, it might claim this position:

- We are experts in the field.

Providing telecommunications consulting to telephone companies, its position could be:

- We're on the leading edge of your industry.

To clarify your firm's position with each of your target markets, complete Worksheet #24. Before you write the summary, take a look at the target market summary in Sample #2 written for Case Inc., a human resources training consultant.

SAMPLE #2
CASE INC. TARGET MARKETS

First target market: Medium-sized (50 – 100 employees) high-tech firms. Many firms in this target group genuinely depend on their employees. They need highly trained people to support research and development.

Few of these firms maintain human resource departments. Most have one person hiring, firing, and coordinating training when he or she has time.

It is important to position service to these firms and personnel administrators to act as a resource that helps keep employees happy and provides quality training so that employees stay with the company.

Second target market: Small- to medium-sized service business (e.g., consulting firms and hotels). These businesses do not have full human resources and training departments either. They depend on their employees to present the best image to clients but they are very concerned about the cost, in time and money, of finding training programs and trainers.

It is important to position our service as a cost-effective way to train employees. We will coordinate training programs for a flat retainer fee that is less than the salary of one person.

---

d. MATCHING OBJECTIVES TO TARGET MARKETS

When you know who you'll serve and how you'll explain the services of your business or professional practice, one final challenge remains in the positioning phase of the marketing plan. Objectives — those quantitative, measurable things your firm will achieve — must now be matched to the target markets you'll serve.

Previously, you specified the marketing changes you wanted to see. Perhaps you determined that, in your car repair business, sales of products such as batteries or tires would increase by 12% over the next year. To achieve that objective, your target market must buy your batteries. Individuals in your target market must buy those tires.

To accomplish your objectives you must assign them to target markets. Doing this may be simple, but likely it will challenge the whole set of goals and objectives you previously set. If, for example, it becomes clear that 12% growth in sales of accessories is too aggressive, the objective must be reduced. However, if the objective in one area is reduced, might it not affect the overall goal for a 25% increase in sales in this year? And if this year's sales goal is reduced, won't that make all the goals for all five years of your projection come tumbling down?

Yes. But also no. Frequently, at this stage, service providers are confronted with the question, "Who will buy this?" or perhaps, "Where will I find time to sell that much more to a target market I've not yet begun to cultivate?"

Although matching your objectives to target markets can be unpleasant because dreams are often forfeited or, more likely, delayed, this exercise does create a set of goals and objectives that are more likely to be achieved. Through modification, refining, distilling, reducing, and compromising comes a better reality — one genuinely possible.

Worksheet #25 will help you match your objectives to your target markets.

WORKSHEET #22
TARGET MARKET IDENTIFICATION

1. Which groups have you decided your firm will target? Identify each with a brief caption.

_____
_____
_____
_____

If your clients are individuals:

2. What are the demographic characteristics of each targeted group?

Target market	Age range	Sex	Race	Family size	Number of adults in the family	Where they live

3. What are the socioeconomic characteristics of each group?

Target market	Level of education	Approximate income	Occupation	Social class

4. Can you identify their lifestyles?

Target market	Activities, interests, beliefs, and opinions

5. Can you determine how frequently they use your service?

Target market	Heavy	Moderate	Light	Never

If your clients are other businesses:

6. What are the characteristics of each group?

Target market	Number of employees	Sales volume ($)	Location	Type of industry

7. Can you determine their buying patterns and how much they buy?

Target market	Heavy	Moderate	Light	Seasonal buying patterns	Size of orders

WORKSHEET #22 — Continued

CHARACTERISTICS OF EACH TARGET MARKET			
Target market: _Sample: Women_	Target market: _____	Target market: _____	Target market: _____
35 – 45 years old			
Professionals			
$50,000+ income			

Now that you have identified your target markets, ask yourself these questions to test your selections.

	Target market: _____	Target market: _____	Target market: _____
1. Is the population of this target market of adequate size to consume your service?			
2. Can the income of this target market support this service?			
3. Does this target market desire this service? How do you know?			
4. Are your competitors already providing this service?			
5. Do you have resources available to serve this market?			

WORKSHEET #24
TARGET MARKET POSITIONING

Determine the position your service now holds and could hold with each target market.

	Target market: _____	Target market: _____	Target market: _____
1. What position does your service have in your prospect's mind?			
2. What position does your company desire over the long term?			
3. What companies must be outdone for you to establish this position?			
4. Does your company have enough resources to occupy and hold this position?			
5. Do you have the tenacity to stick with a consistent positioning strategy?			
6. Does your company's creative approach (e.g., brochures, signs, and logo) match your positioning strategy?			

TARGET MARKET SUMMARY

Summarize here the target markets you have identified and the results of your target market test and positioning.

_____

_____

_____

_____

_____

_____

_____

_____

_____

_____

_____

_____

_____

_____

_____

_____

_____

_____

_____

_____

_____

_____

_____

_____

_____

_____

_____

_____

_____

WORKSHEET #25
OBJECTIVES AND TARGET MARKETS

1. Assign the objective you developed in Worksheet #21 to the target markets you've just identified.

   Target market: _____

   Objective: _____

   _____

   Objective: _____

   _____

   Target market: _____

   Objective: _____

   _____

   Objective: _____

   _____

   Target market: _____

   Objective: _____

   _____

   Objective: _____

   _____

2. Are there objectives you set earlier that now need to be modified to reach your target markets? _____

   _____

   _____

   _____

   _____

   _____

   _____

3. How would you change these objectives?

Original objective:_____

_____

_____

_____

Change(s): _____

_____

_____

_____

Original objective:_____

_____

_____

_____

Change(s): _____

_____

_____

_____

Original objective:_____

_____

_____

_____

Change(s): _____

_____

_____

_____

_____

4. Now apply each changed objective to a target market.

Target market: _____

Objective: _____

_____

_____

Objective: _____

_____

_____

Target market: _____

Objective: _____

_____

_____

Objective: _____

_____

_____

Target market: _____

Objective: _____

_____

_____

Objective: _____

_____

_____

OBJECTIVES AND TARGET MARKETS SUMMARY

Summarize your conclusions about how your objectives fit your target markets.

_____

_____

_____

_____

_____

_____

_____

_____

_____

_____

_____

_____

_____

_____

_____

_____

_____

_____

_____

_____

_____

_____

_____

_____

_____

_____

_____

11
STRATEGIES

a. STRATEGIES: OPPORTUNITY FOR ACTION

Thus far in preparing the marketing plan for your service business or professional practice, you have viewed goals in association with your objectives, target markets, and market position. In doing so, you have aligned your firm to achieve those goals.

Getting to this step in the planning process has probably been useful. Now you can be specific about *what* will be done *when* by *whom* and act on your marketing plan.

It may help to think of the process you have completed as a funnel.

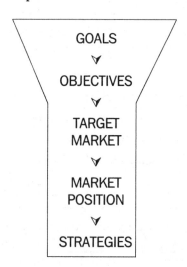

Strategies, the product of the funnel, are important to your marketing plan in the following ways:

- Strategies spell out how to achieve your objectives.

- Strategies are established for each part of the marketing mix: services, fees, the way services are distributed, and how those services are promoted to your clients.

- Strategies consider what your company will do, when, where, and with what tools.

- Strategies evaluate the internal costs to your firm, identifying time, staff, and financial resources.

When you develop strategies, remember first to *always* respond to client needs and desires. Use everything you know, believe, or even suspect about your target markets to help you set responsive service, fee, and method strategies. Then, adopt promotion strategies. Since promotion carries your company's message to its target markets, you must clarify every other marketing aspect before you plan to promote those services, fees, or methods.

Develop strategies around the needs of your target market, like this:

110

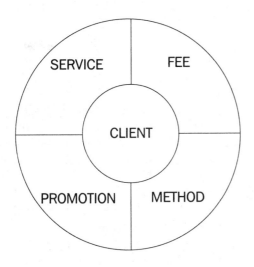

Finally, prioritize different strategies if you find they fragment your efforts, and those of your associates, to serve clients. For example, you may be ready to offer several new services but realize that having to learn too many new service skills will weaken your staff's ability to be expert at each one. Therefore, choose one service, develop it completely, offer it, and carefully analyze how long it takes to become accepted and how well it is accepted. Then move on to the next service idea.

b. SERVICE STRATEGIES

Only three kinds of strategies might be developed for your services. Each strategy may seem simple, but new services can profoundly affect your firm, so set service strategies with caution.

Your service strategies might include the following:

- Adding a service
- Modifying an existing service
- Eliminating one or more services

The first strategy requires the most internal resources, creates the greatest risk, and takes the longest time. (Bankers say, accurately, that adding a new service takes twice as long and costs twice as much.) The last strategy has an impact on people — both staff and clients — the most. Yet, service providers often decide on these two when, in fact, improving an existing service in a way that responds best to the clients might make the greatest impact — with the least risk. To set these strategies, ask yourself this question: "Which strategy would help me best serve the needs, desires, or wishes of my clients?"

One experienced consultant to the utilities industry asked herself that question. She discovered that her clients wanted to be able to measure the effectiveness of their customer service efforts. So she established a strategy of working with a colleague to develop a customer audit for these utilities. Because she chose to work on this audit while continuing to serve clients through ongoing training and consulting work, development required two years. By the time the audit was complete, tested with a utility, and announced, three years had passed, but her clients were served in the best way possible.

c. FEE STRATEGIES

Generally, four kinds of strategies are developed for fee schedules:

- *Skim the cream off the market.* Set a high price. It works only if your service is innovative, in demand, and has no competition. An example is an engineering firm that specializes in rearranging elements of construction projects so that building costs are reduced and projects completed on schedule.

- *Competitive pricing.* If the service is one of several comparable services in a growing market, set the market price. An example is an image consulting firm that offers individual and corporate seminars on dress and presentation.

- *Market penetration.* A lower price is set to create a mass market for a service that is highly sensitive to price (such as hair designers or financial consulting).

- *Pre-emptive pricing.* Deliberately price at a low level to discourage potential competition. For example, the consulting arm of a large accounting firm once bid a $100,000 project at $10,000 to maintain its dominance in the regional hospital market.

Any pricing strategy must be seen within the context of the overall survival of the firm. Fees *must* be linked to overall goals and objectives. Are you trying to maximize profits, recover costs, or what? Make certain your pricing strategies contribute to long-term goals.

d. DISTRIBUTION STRATEGIES

Usually, strategies determining the place from which you'll serve your clients are concrete, while the way your firm will serve them may be more abstract and innovative. You might consider the following:

- Change your current office or outlet.

- Expand the number of places from which you'll offer your service.

- Change the way your clients reach you, or vice versa.

- Use or motivate middle people, such as marketing representatives and brokers.

Generally, the first two strategies require large capital investments. The last two require less money but demand more creativity, time, and energy. They take advantage of opportunities, which abound in this era of marketing change, for new ways of providing service to clients. Sometimes, one strategy will improve both the *place* from which the service is distributed and the *way* it is distributed. For example, a group of ophthalmologists completely redesigned their clinic. In the surgical quarters, they had a glass wall added so relatives could watch eye surgery being done. The special room introduced a new way of better serving the patient.

Technology can improve the way you serve your clients. The owner of a printing company knows this when he invests in state-of-the art equipment for printing "direct to plate." Other simpler strategies, such as a training firm deciding to offer seminars only within major corporations, can profoundly affect the business too.

e. PROMOTIONAL STRATEGIES

Promotion, a huge area of marketing, is also very complex for service providers. There are all kinds of ways your firm can get the word out to its target markets about its services. Although the field of promoting service businesses is an emerging one, numerous tools are already available to service providers. In fields with little marketing history (e.g., medicine, law, and accounting), a more limited range of tools can be used. Other disciplines (e.g., consulting or training) have few restrictions beyond good taste. For others, which require a storefront operation (e.g., hair salons), the standard promotional techniques may work well.

Service providers will seek the proper mix of promotional tools to take from the marketing toolbox. In many businesses, the personal style of the service provider will differentiate which promotional tools are used. Some people enjoy those tools that put them (usually talking happily) in front of other people. Some prefer activities that do not involve personal contact. Skills (e.g., speaking in front of groups or writing) make a difference as well. Within the guidelines for promotion that follow, such preferences are to be encouraged.

The following promotional tools are most effective for any service business or professional practice. We call their use "personal contact marketing," because it is clear that promoting and selling a service is done best by telling others about a service through direct or indirect contact. The tools are —

- Referrals
- Client relations
- Selling
- Public speaking
- Participation in organizations
- Direct mail (of material such as a newsletter or an offer for a discount on services)
- The Internet
- Telemarketing
- Publicity (e.g., free or mass media; not to be confused with paid advertising)
- Special promotional items
- Advertising

1. Referrals

Referrals are most successfully generated by two groups of people: satisfied clients who have used the service and professional colleagues. To elicit a continuing stream of referrals, you'll find that these "four R's" work best.

- *Request the referral.* Referrals are not necessarily a result of doing excellent work (though most service providers fervently hope so). The words must be spoken aloud: "This is what we do, and this is who we serve. If you know of anyone who has a problem like this, would you be willing to tell them about us?" (Almost everyone says yes.)

- *Repeat the request.* Send materials to those who need them to help them make referrals. This might include a brochure, a professional or company profile, a list of services, past clients, or testimonial letters. Include a note, thanking them for agreeing to refer prospective clients. Call back a week or so later to ensure that there are no more questions. Put them on your company's mailing list, and check in with them from time to time. (No, they won't think you're a pest, because you're a nice person, you don't ask them to refer business to you every time you call back, and, by the information you share, you add to their pool of knowledge, thus giving something back to them.)

- *Reward referrals.* It's basic behaviorism: the behavior you reward increases. Too often, you don't know what happens when you refer a prospect to an associate. But when that associate thanks you, you'll do it again. And again! Be an exception in your field: thank the people who support you, by a phone call or a note, with a lunch or dinner, or with a beautiful plant or bouquet of spring flowers. Increase the size of the reward with the number of referrals. You cannot, of course, offer money — finder's fees — to some professionals, including licensed practitioners such as doctors and lawyers. Neither should money be exchanged if the reward would in any way seem unethical, as between interior designers and manufacturers' representatives. You must also be careful not to reveal confidential client or patient information with your "thank you."

- *Reciprocate.* The most important way to increase referrals is to send them to others who are supporting you. You'll demonstrate that you're willing to give back what others have given you and, more important, you'll provide high quality service to clients.

2. Client relations

Recent reading, research, and work with our clients has convinced us that they often can't tell how competent the people who serve them are. As well, unless professionals produce incompetent work, it may not even matter to their clients. What makes a difference to them is how they are treated. Therefore, *bond* the client to your service business or professional practice emotionally. In competitive fields, bonding becomes even more important.

Client relations doesn't mean hype or dishonesty. It's more successful, in fact, if this simple formula is adhered to: consistent courtesy + common sense + professional dignity = effective client relations.

Client relations is first the job of support staff. The hair salon manager or the medical office receptionist who greets clients on the phone may be even more important than the person who actually delivers the service. That individual's telephone presence and his or her kindness to those who visit the office provide the first impression — the one with the most impact.

Some aspects of the service provider's client relations role are obvious; others are subtle. Respecting your clients by being on time and greeting them as though they were being hosted in your home are obvious aspects of good client relations. More subtle is counseling the whole person by listening to the emotions as well as the problem you'll help the client solve. Also subtle is the approach that treats clients as equals.

Respect the client's expertise, work as an equal with the client, and, together, solve the client's problem. Report frequently on work that takes a long time to complete (e.g., architect's design, legal case, engine overhaul, medical diagnosis), even when there is nothing new to report. Show a personal interest in the client beyond the professional relationship (e.g., send flowers to a client's business opening, inquire about a recent vacation, comment on his or her excellent appearance, buy his or her products or services). You may develop the ultimate bond. If the person is good enough to be your client, he or she is good enough to care about and buy from.

3. Selling a service

To sell a service as a professional, listen before you talk and control the sales interview by asking questions. Unlike those who sell a particular product, you can adapt your service to a prospective client's needs and thus operate your firm in a genuinely creative way.

The sales approach that works well for people in services is the consultant model, or relationship selling. This involves three steps:

- Discovering the desired outcome
- Matching your service to it
- Gaining the client's commitment

In the sales contact, 50% of the time with the prospective client needs to be spent discussing his or her expectations about the outcome of your service. This is accomplished by establishing rapport or aligning yourself with the client, questioning (via open-ended who, what, when, where, and how questions), and using active listening skills.

Once the need, problem, and expectations are determined, it's possible to personalize your service to the client's need. This gives the client a sense that you understand the need and are responding directly to it.

If done genuinely and conversationally, gaining commitment to your service is as simple as asking, "What else do you need to feel comfortable about getting started on the project?"

4. Public speaking

One of the most effective ways to reach new prospective clients is to deliver a public presentation of some kind. But there's a catch. First, you must talk chiefly to your target market or to primary referral sources (as when lawyers refer to lawyers). Second, you must do it very well.

For the short-run, prepare carefully, practice, and record a practice session. To build skills for the long-term, join an organization, such as Toastmasters, that trains speakers. Third, unless you're a trainer, subtly find a way to help members of your audience understand that you offer individual services and are available to serve them. Offering a free half-hour consultation or a discount on a lube job can do it.

Don't wait to be asked. Come up with an interesting topic. In the Yellow Pages, look up clubs, organizations, and professional associations. Identify those whose membership might include prospective clients and call the program directors of those organizations. Send your brochure, your credentials as a speaker, and a paragraph describing your talk. Be politely persistent.

If your industry holds trade shows, consider having a booth at the best show in your market area. Your booth must be top quality, in an excellent location, and unusual in some way. Urge employees who staff the booth to be salespeople, not custodians. Come out of the show with qualified leads for your staff to follow up on within ten days.

5. Participation in organizations

Joining just two organizations of people who might be prospective clients can provide both referrals and new business. Ask associates which organizations might be most suitable for you. Visit the organizations before you decide to join.

When you invest this way, expect to devote time before your investment in the group pays off. Meanwhile, build your reputation in the group. Ask the president about exciting projects and volunteer for those that have visibility in the group. Treat the volunteer job like a great professional opportunity and produce results for the group. Offer to report for your committee to the entire organization. Finally, after you've made your mark, lunch individually with the president and other influential officers; tell them what you do and ask for referrals in a low-key way. As the group's trendsetters, they'll pass the word along to others.

We suggest that you limit your membership to two groups because many service providers find they are unable to contribute to more than two groups at one time.

6. Direct mail

Sending direct mail pieces to your clientele may be one of the most effective ways to market your service business or professional practice *if* this expensive method is used properly. The first step is to mail to the right people. Your best mailing list includes those who know your company: current clients, professional associates, prospective clients, even friends. This list should be updated at least once a year.

You may choose to rent or buy mailing lists of prospects who do not know about your firm, but expect the response to be lower. For example, if a mailer to your list of known clients generates responses from 5% of those who receive the mailing (the usual response), you should expect that a mailing to those who do not know you will generate less than a 2% response.

Almost as important as the mailing list is what you offer. If you mail a newsletter — an excellent strategy for professionals because it reveals the depth and breadth of your knowledge about the field — what you offer is really information. Direct response is not usually expected, although after about four excellent newsletters, it often comes.

A more aggressive marketing effort is a mailing that offers a free service (e.g., revising an existing will) or a discount off the regular price of a service (e.g., 10% off the price of a weight reducing program in January). That offer should be expressed in a letter, which is expertly written and explains the results customers will get. Include testimonials, and be very explicit about how the person who receives the offer can respond.

Marry your direct mail piece to another promotional technique, such as telemarketing, conducted after a mailer is sent. If direct mail is new to you, you may want to enlist the services of a firm specializing in this discipline.

7. The Internet

The Internet, a global network of interconnected computers, provides another venue to promote your business: the Web site. The Web site is a page (or pages) of information about your business and its service that can be created either personally — if you are "Net savvy" — or by a professional Web developer, who will charge a fee for his or her services. If you've spent any time at all on the Internet, you will know that Web sites range from those using straight text to ones incorporating music, video, photographic images, and sophisticated graphics.

When your Web site is built, it is uploaded to the Internet "highway" where anyone using the Net can stop by. Once there, they may read about your business and service and move on, e-mail you for more information, or place an order.

The paradox of the Web site is that it needs to be promoted itself. Building it is easy; the challenge is getting noticed. It needs the support of other media. Your Web site's Internet address, known as a URL (Uniform Resource Locator), should be prominent on all your brochures, flyers, business cards, and any other promotional material you use for your service.

The other route to your site is via links to the various Internet search engines. AltaVista, Yahoo, Infoseek, Webcrawler, and Lycos are some examples of search engines. Given some key words, these programs sweep the World Wide Web (WWW), identify Web sites containing those words, and list them. If the person keys in words that are prominent in your site, your URL will be listed for viewing — along with hundreds of others. Most of the search programs, after asking you to read a few do's and don'ts, make linking up a simple matter.

The Internet is not paved with gold, so don't expect hundreds of new clients to come knocking on your door overnight. The Net has a strong commercial presence and business *is* being done there, but it is not one big shopping mall with customers throwing money at every new offering. Despite this, and because businesspeople are drawn to a potentially global market, the Web site is now a key component in most companies' promotional and marketing programs.

Don't rush headlong onto this very special "highway." A poor Web presence, over-hyped and ill-conceived, will accomplish nothing for you or your business. Do take some thoughtful steps.

Spend some time on the Internet, either with a helpful colleague familiar with computers or through an Internet service provider. Check out numerous sites and try talking, via e-mail, to the site hosts. Many of them will be happy to give you tips and pointers on what works and what doesn't.

8. Telemarketing

Telemarketing is a disciplined, planned campaign of using the telephone to sell, or initiate the sale of, services. The calls are made by well-prepared, skilled callers. Properly executed, a telemarketing campaign can reap considerable returns for the business using it — and it serves the client as well. Calling customers of a hair salon to schedule a trim or checking back to see if a photocopier needs servicing are two excellent strategies. Telemarketing can be used more in some service businesses than in others. As with direct mail, your best audience may be current customers or known potential ones. But telemarketing has also been used successfully to set up an initial in-person appointment with a new prospect.

Telemarketing depends heavily on both the script and the individuals who do the phoning. The script should take into account all possible responses; use it to guide the interviewer through the call during training. Interviewers should be chosen for their intelligence, enthusiasm, persistence, courteous manner, and ability to react quickly on the phone.

9. Publicity

Unlike advertising, which is paid promotion, publicity is free. Though both are carried in the mass media, publicity is generally considered more believable. An article one of your firm's specialists or a reporter writes about the work your firm does can lay a foundation of credibility and recognition. Occasionally, it will produce business as well, though this is less frequent.

To generate publicity about your firm, first seek out the publications that serve your target market. You may be tempted to have your photograph in your city's local daily newspaper, but first find out if this is the publication the decision makers in your target market read. If not, identify the trade or industry publications they read. Then, generate a story idea that is different and even a little controversial. Contact a reporter whose articles you respect and propose the story idea, explaining why it will interest the publication's readers. Before the interview, jot down 10 points you want to make during the discussion. Speak from the readers' perspective, and explain why your story is important to them. Don't hesitate to explain that you know about the story through your work with clients in the field. Don't say anything you don't want to see in print, and don't give answers to hypothetical questions. Have a black and white glossy photograph available; articles with photographs receive readership 20 times as great as those without photos. When the article is published, send reprints to your mailing list. It will remind clients, associates, prospective clients, and friends about your firm's services and further establish your credibility as a leader in your field.

10. Special promotional items

Don't overlook an excellent tangible reminder of your intangible services: a promotional item. You are probably most familiar with such specialty items as pens printed with the company name or a realtor's car litter bag. Today, however, more sophisticated promotional items can serve even engineers or accountants. You can select a small item, such as a pen in an attractive holder, which can be given to everyone. Or you might choose a more expensive item, such as an elegant crystal paperweight, to give to special clients. Whether you choose an expensive or inexpensive item, presenting it with pride to the recipient will enhance its value.

11. Advertising

The decision about whether to advertise should depend on these factors:

- how your clients find you;
- where they are located;
- which newspapers, magazines, or broadcasters serve them; and
- the cost of advertising.

If you don't know which media your clients use, ask them through a simple market survey *before* you advertise. Carefully select the media outlets you'll use. Ask for a publication's reader profile and match it with your target market's demographics before taking out an ad. Plan on advertising repeatedly. Advertising research indicates that at least six repetitions of the same message are needed to make some members of your target market aware of your services.

Even the conservative informational ads required in the legal and medical professions should be carefully designed to appeal to your audience. Producing the ads and placing them in the proper media usually require the services of professionals in this field.

f. PROMOTION RULES

The preceding plethora of choices may produce more confusion than clarity. It may seem that there are just too many tools in the toolbox. Here are some rules to help simplify the complex world of promotion.

1. Promotion must be planned

Service business owners and principals in professional firms are usually so busy delivering the service or managing those who do that they rarely think about promoting — until the wolf, instead of a new client, is at the door. A simple calendar marked with what promotional activities you'll undertake in which months is an excellent strategy; it helps the firm keep making the promotional investments that pay off in new clients.

2. Promotion can be creative

Promotional efforts are often more effective if they take a slight creative risk, one that does not violate the informal rules of its profession but creates interest and, perhaps, has a little fun at the same time.

A warning: creativity fades as stress increases. Don't wait until you have no clients before you create a new promotional idea. It's too late, too expensive, and too difficult. Instead, plan the year's promotion with your staff, drawing on the positive effects of group interaction. Retreat for a day to brainstorm ideas. Leave the list of ideas on the coffee room bulletin board for a week while everybody adds to it.

For example, emulate one shrewd, successful gas station owner who took his employees to dinner every few months to toss around ideas. Good ideas emerged between the soup and the nuts.

3. Promotion is labor-intensive

You call Dr. Jones because someone who receives her newsletter told you she is a great dentist. You are impressed by Kay's hairstyling expertise at a demonstration, and you make an appointment to change your hairstyle. You take your car to Bob because he's an honest, experienced mechanic and a great guy you met at a luncheon club meeting.

Dr. Jones, Kay, and Bob have learned perhaps the hardest lesson of promoting a service business: it is as labor-intensive as providing the service itself. The smaller the company, the truer this rule: it is the individual's service you choose, not just the firm's. Even in large firms, this is the case. Thus, every service provider must integrate promotion into his or her job description, rather than depend on the rainmaker, as the business-generating partner in law firms is called.

4. Promotion must be varied and continuous

Marketing experts generally agree that it is impossible to measure the success of each promotional effort. But they also agree that different stimuli prompt different clients to use any service. Therefore, don't stop when a promotion seems successful; continue with another, then another, until a variety of clients are reached. Take out a hammer and a screwdriver and a saw from the promotional toolbox; one tool is not enough.

Because no one promotional tool serves all needs, the question to be answered is which combination works best. Three guidelines will help you design the promotion mix that makes the most impact.

- *Combine known and new.* Does the audience of the intended promotional effort know about your firm? Or is it hearing about your business for the first time? Successful promotion combines both new and known audiences. (Businesses cannot succeed by drawing just on known clientele.)

- *Use in-person and other promotion.* Is the promotion, like Kay's demonstration, in-person? Or like Dr. Jones's newsletter, another kind of promotion? In-person promotion may be four to five times more effective. However, because of the labor-intensive nature of both the work and the promotion of service businesses, a delicate balance must be maintained between those activities that "get the work" and those that allow you to "do the work."

Use one-time and repetitious promotion. Is the promotion a one-time effort to meet prospective clients, like meeting Bob at the luncheon? Or is it repetitious, like the newsletter, reminding prospects of your knowledge and expertise? Again, both must be integrated into your promotion plan.

g. WRITING STRATEGIES

After considering possible strategies in the areas of service, fee, place, and promotion, it's time now to determine the strategies you need to meet your goals and objectives: what specifically will you do and when, where, how, and with what tools will you do it? As a start, answer the questions in Worksheet #26. Then use Worksheet #27 to write your strategies for achieving the objectives you have set for each target market. (Three blank worksheets are provided; if you need more, you may photocopy those worksheets.) Use the strategy in Sample #3 as a guide for writing your strategies. You should also think about the impact each strategy will have on the internal workings of your company.

h. TESTING STRATEGIES

To write a strategy is one thing; to produce the kind of results you want is something else. Test your strategies on Worksheet #28.

120

SERVICE

1. Might you retain the services your company currently sells?

   ❏ Yes   ❏ No

2. Why would you make this decision?

   _____

   _____

   _____

3. Might you add to your company's service line?

   ❏ Yes   ❏ No

4. Why? _____

   _____

   _____

5. If you might add a service, subject the service idea to these rigorous tests:

Evaluation factors	Amounts			Reasons for evaluation
	Small	Moderate	Large	
Financial resources required				
Market potential				
Competitive services				
Research and development required				
Production time and costs				
Sales and distribution complexity				
Legal problems				

6. Have you carefully considered ways to overcome these common reasons new services fail?
   - Poor timing
   - Poor information about competitors
   - Changed client needs
   - New service incompatible with rest of company's line
   - Impractical service
   - Service competing with clients' sales
   - Bad market analysis
   - Disparity between demand for new service and its supply

7. Might you consider modifying your service?
   ❑ Yes   ❑ No

8. If so, would you do this?
   ❑ Yes   ❑ No

9. What specifically might you change about the service?
   The service quality _____
   Service _____
   Other (specify): _____

10. How might it be more attractive to clients or benefit them more after modification?
    _____
    _____
    _____

11. Might you decide to drop a current service?
    ❑ Yes   ❑ No

12. Why would you make this decision?

_____

_____

_____

13. When might you eliminate the service? (Describe in detail.)

_____

_____

_____

14. What could be your interim plans while the service is being phased out?
   - ❑ Maintain current level of promotion
   - ❑ Reduce promotion
   - ❑ Eliminate promotion
   - ❑ Maintain price
   - ❑ Lower price
   - ❑ Raise price

FEES

1. Might you retain current fees for the services your company offers?
   - ❑ Yes   ❑ No

2. Why would you make this decision?

_____

_____

_____

3. If you might decide to change the service, what change could you make?

Increase fees _____ Decrease fees_____

Other (specify): _____

4. What would this change accomplish? _____
_____
_____

5. Would this be a permanent price change, or a temporary change (as in the case of seasonal sales or inventory clearances)?
_____
_____
_____

6. If the fee change is temporary, when might it begin and for how long might it be effective? _____
_____
_____

7. Might your company continue your current credit policies or adapt them?
_____
_____
_____

8. Why might you make this decision? _____
_____
_____

9. Why might you adapt your credit policies, if that is your decision?
_____
_____
_____

10. When might you make the change, and how could you introduce it?

_____

_____

_____

11. Are discounts appropriate for your business?
    ❏ Yes   ❏ No

12. Which type of discount?
    ❏ Cash   ❏ Quantity   ❏ Promotion

13. How might you implement the appropriate discount, and when?

_____

_____

_____

_____

PLACE

1. Do your current premises meet your needs and those of your clients?
    ❏ Yes   ❏ No

2. If not, would you change your company's place of business?
    ❏ Yes   ❏ No

3. What type of change might you make?

    Move to another location? (specify): _____

_____

_____

Make physical changes in current location(s)? (specify): _____

_____

_____

_____

4. When could this change take place?

_____

_____

_____

5. Why would you decide on this change?

_____

_____

_____

6. Could you make changes in the way your company serves its clients?

❑ Yes ❑ No

Explain: _____

_____

7. What changes might you make? _____

_____

_____

8. How would the changes you might make enable you to serve your clients better?

_____

_____

_____

9. If you might make such a change, have you considered the research needed?

- Compare the cost of changes (e.g., transportation) with profits.
- Assess whether legal problems may arise.
- Commit only to arrangements that give your company as much flexibility as possible.
- Make a time commitment that meets your company's goals, as well as those of other parties.

PROMOTIONS

1. What promotion tools do you favor for your business?

   ❑ Direct sales   ❑ Web site

   ❑ Referrals   ❑ Sales promotion

   ❑ Client relations   ❑ Advertising

   ❑ Participation in organizations   ❑ Public speaking

   ❑ Direct mail   ❑ Telemarketing

2. Why do you favor these tools?

   _____

   _____

   _____

   _____

   _____

3. Are these the tools you've been using in your business?

   ❑ Yes   ❑ No

   Explain: _____

   _____

   _____

   _____

WORKSHEET #26 — Continued

4. How might you begin using the promotional tools you identified in question #1?

_____

_____

_____

_____

_____

5. How would your target markets respond to these types of promotions? Particularly, would they be more likely to buy your service if you used these promotions?

_____

_____

_____

_____

_____

6. If so, when would you use these promotions?

_____

_____

_____

_____

_____

7. How much would using these promotions cost in terms of staff time, as well as money?

_____

_____

_____

_____

_____

➤ **TARGET MARKET #1:** _____

Objectives that relate to this target market:

    1._____

    2._____

    3._____

Strategies needed to achieve these objectives:

Marketing mix

    • Customer_____

    _____

    • Place (distribution) _____

    _____

    • Price_____

    _____

    • Promotion

        Direct sales: _____

        Publicity: _____

        Referrals: _____

        Client relations: _____

        Participation in organizations: _____

        Direct mail:_____

        Web site: _____

        Sales promotions: _____

        Advertising:_____

        Public speaking:_____

        Telemarketing: _____

Internal considerations

- Amount of time strategies will require:_____
_____

- Costs of strategies: _____
_____

- Staff required by strategies: _____
_____

➢ **TARGET MARKET #2:** _____

Objectives that relate to this target market:

1._____
2._____
3._____

Strategies needed to achieve these objectives:
Marketing mix

- Customer_____
_____

- Place (distribution) _____
_____

- Price_____
_____

- Promotion
  Direct sales: _____
  Publicity: _____
  Referrals: _____
  Client relations: _____
  Participation in organizations: _____

Direct mail:_____

Web site: _____

Sales promotions: _____

Advertising:_____

Public speaking:_____

Telemarketing: _____

Internal considerations

- Amount of time strategies will require:_____

_____

- Costs of strategies: _____

_____

- Staff required by strategies: _____

_____

➢ **TARGET MARKET #3:** _____

Objectives that relate to this target market:

1._____

2._____

3._____

Strategies needed to achieve these objectives:

Marketing mix

- Customer_____

_____

- Place (distribution) _____

_____

- Price_____

  _____

- Promotion

  Direct sales: _____

  Publicity: _____

  Referrals: _____

  Client relations: _____

  Participation in organizations: _____

  Direct mail:_____

  Web site: _____

  Sales promotions: _____

  Advertising: _____

  Public speaking:_____

  Telemarketing: _____

Internal considerations

- Amount of time strategies will require:_____

  _____

- Costs of strategies: _____

  _____

- Staff required by strategies: _____

  _____

> **TARGET MARKET:** Medium-sized businesses

Objectives that relate to this target market:

1. Acquire two new clients by year-end.

2. Increase income 10% by September.

3. Solicit five referrals from existing clients within three months.

Strategies needed to achieve these objectives:

Marketing mix

- Client: Build contacts with existing customers and identify new potential business within market.

- Place (distribution): Determine ways to make it easier for clients to access our services — deliver more workshops on site, upgrade telephone system, develop Web site.

- Fee: Convert from hourly fee to fee for value, project fee or retainer according to client needs.

- Promotion:

  Direct sales: Increase sales efforts. Train staff in selling.

  Publicity: Develop an active publicity campaign in selected journals.

  Referrals: Solicit referrals from existing clients. Make contacts with other referral sources.

  Client relations: Install a client satisfaction program. After each project, evaluate our work with client.

  Participation in organizations: Join selective professional and business organizations so that we meet new clients.

Direct mail: Upgrade brochure. (No other approach.)

Web site: Work with Internet service provider to develop Internet presence.

Sales promotions: None.

Advertising: Limited advertising through Yellow Pages and chamber of commerce membership directory.

Public speaking: Actively solicit speaking engagements from groups that are related to our market.

Telemarketing: Train staff on phone techniques — not for solicitation but for handling inquiries.

Internal considerations

- Amount of time strategies will require: Considerable amount of key partners' time because strategies are personally oriented.

- Costs of strategies: Training — investment

    Brochure — investment

- Staff required by strategies: Minimal except for training. Key partners will invest most time in following up with clients and in planning strategies.

1. List your service strategies	Are your rushing a revolutionary service to market?	Must your company produce a new service?

2. List your fee strategies	Does the strategy balance the minimum risk with the maximum profit potential?	

3. List your place strategies	Does the strategy take you too far from current services and markets?	Is the strategy appropriate, given existing and prospective physical facilities?

WORKSHEET #28 — Continued

4. List your promotion strategies	Does this strategy reach your client most effectively?	Are you comfortable with this promotion strategy?

5. Ask the following questions of each strategy.
  - Is the strategy realistic?

  _____

  _____

  _____

  _____

  _____

  - What are the implications of allocating money to this single strategy?

  _____

  _____

  _____

  _____

  _____

  - Is too much capital and management tied to this strategy?

  _____

  _____

  _____

  _____

  _____

  - Does the strategy fit a market niche not filled by others?

  _____

  _____

  _____

  _____

  _____

- Will that market niche be open long enough to return both capital investment and profit?

  _____

  _____

  _____

  _____

  _____

- Is the strategy legal, moral, and ethical?

  _____

  _____

  _____

  _____

  _____

- Do the strategies interrelate?

  _____

  _____

  _____

  _____

  _____

- Does the strategy exploit your company's strengths and avoid its weaknesses?

  _____

  _____

  _____

  _____

  _____

THE MARKETING ACTION PLAN 12

a. STEPPING INTO ACTION

When your firm's strategies are determined, you are ready to organize all your efforts into an action plan. Organization is the function of an action plan. An action plan is a tool for setting priorities. It is a schedule of specific activities needed to fulfill each of your strategies. Its importance cannot be overemphasized. This plan summarizes everything you will do to market your business, in what order, and when.

Creating a complete action plan, which we recommend, requires the following five critical steps:

(a) Articulate your strategies.

(b) Determine your budget.

(c) Combine the strategies with the budget to get an annual marketing budget.

(d) Set an immediate, detailed quarterly budget.

(e) Assess how well the plan is coordinated.

Your first challenge is to think through each strategy in detail. To do so, you need to understand the difference between a *strategy* and an *activity*. Activities are the finite parts of strategies. For example,

"producing a brochure" is a strategy, not an activity. To produce a brochure requires activities such as writing, designing, producing, and printing. Administrative steps, such as approving the text and design, may also be required.

To describe each activity, you must think through each strategy in detail. Ask what steps (or activities) are required to accomplish the strategy. List those activities in order. Which logically comes first and last?

Many people find that arranging these activities on a flow chart, such as the one in Worksheet #29, expedites this process. Simply write down each activity in order, using as many of the boxes in the flow chart as necessary. When you have listed them all, put the date you want that strategy completed in the last box. Working back from that date, set dates for each activity. Later, after you complete the budget, you may want to note the cost of each activity on the flow chart.

b. BUDGETING MARKETING COSTS

To produce an action plan that will be implemented requires considering not just activities but their costs. The costs also frequently have an impact on the schedule.

139

For each activity you've described, you need to know the costs you'll incur. The following are among the categories of budget items often incurred in marketing budgets.

- Personnel: salaries, personnel benefits, consultants' fees
- Travel and transportation: staff travel, consultants' travel
- Postage and shipping
- Rent, communications, and utilities: facility rental, equipment rental, telephone, and utilities
- Printing and duplication
- Supplies and materials: office supplies, printed materials
- Other services: data processing, subcontracts, conference expenses

Using Worksheet #30, calculate the costs of each activity. These costs can be estimated if you or someone on your staff is familiar with marketing costs. Otherwise, take time to solicit at least two estimates from reputable suppliers.

c. COMBINING ACTIVITIES AND BUDGET INTO AN ACTION PLAN

With activities defined, along with the costs of those activities, you are ready to combine the two into the action plan for your firm.

You'll find that you are now awash in paper. Do not despair. The masses of flow charts and activities and budget worksheets will shortly be reduced to just a few.

From your flow charts, list the proposed activities in date order. Incorporate the costs of each activity. Note the start and finish dates of the activity. Also, insert a date you'll want to check back, a date to make certain that the activity is progressing well. Look at the action plan in Sample #4 before completing Worksheet #31.

d. PREPARING A QUARTERLY BUDGET

With a budget developed from details of the activities you plan, you should have sufficient information to develop an entire marketing budget. You can choose an annual budget, but a detailed quarterly budget provides the greatest direction as you work to implement your plan.

To prepare your budget, combine the cost projections of similar activities. For example, total all your advertising costs and identify when in the budget year they will occur. Worksheet #32 will help you budget your marketing costs.

e. BEFORE IMPLEMENTATION BEGINS

Before you implement your marketing plan, take a few moments to assess its viability. Make certain that this new babe, so long in the womb, can survive in the world. Your marketing plan will work if it fits your firm and its environment. Such coordination — considered after activities and costs are identified — is essential. It lets you test the internal fit. How well will the plan be accepted by individuals in the firm? Will it work with your financial wherewithal? In addition, it challenges you to consider external factors, such as market conditions and the competition. Use Worksheet #33 as a checklist.

140

Strategy: _____

Proposed start date: _____

Deadline for completion: _____

| Activity:

 Date: _____
 Cost: $ _____ | ⇨ | Activity:

 Date: _____
 Cost: $ _____ | ⇨ |

| Activity:

 Date: _____
 Cost: $ _____ | ⇨ | Activity:

 Date: _____
 Cost: $ _____ | ⇨ |

| Activity:

 Date: _____
 Cost: $ _____ | ⇨ | Activity:

 Date: _____
 Cost: $ _____ | ⇨ |

| Activity:

 Date: _____
 Cost: $ _____ | ⇨ | Activity:

 Date: _____
 Cost: $ _____ |

141

WORKSHEET #30
ACTIVITIES AND BUDGETS

Strategy: _____

Action to be taken	Dates	Description	Time/cost requirements	Amount	Budget category

List actions in the order they will be taken.	Cost of each action	Starting date	Check back date	Completion date
1. Develop list of key clients for referrals	2 – 3 hours	8/1	8/10	8/15
2. Develop list of potential referral sources	4 – 6 hours	8/1	8/15	8/20
3. Identify new target clients	3 – 4 hours	8/1	8/5	8/10
4. Investigate potential sales training	4 – 8 hours	8/1	8/15	8/30
5. Train staff	$2,000 – 3,000	9/1	9/15	9/30
6. Contact referral sources and clients	2 – 3 hours per week	9/1	monthly	ongoing
7. Interview PR consulting firms; decide on one	4 hours	9/15	9/30	10/15
8. Determine costs and options for advertising	$100 – 150 per month	10/1	11/1	11/30
9. Develop list of potential speaking engagements	8 hours	8/15	8/31	9/10
10. Begin contacting groups	8+ hours	9/10	10/5	11/1
11. Investigate organizations to join	$500 – 1,000 + 8 hours	9/1	10/1	11/1
12. Contact professionalre: brochure	$5,000 – 6,000	9/1	10/1	11/1
13.				
14.				
15.				

WORKSHEET #31
MARKETING ACTION PLAN

List actions in the order they will be taken	Cost of each action	Starting date	Check back date	Completion date
1.				
2.				
3.				
4.				
5.				
6.				
7.				
8.				
9.				
10.				
11.				
12.				
13.				
14.				
15.				

	Quarter			
	First	**Second**	**Third**	**Fourth**
Marketing expenditures				
Promotional techniques				
Direct mail				
Web site				
Referral lunches				
Telemarketing				
Materials for speeches				
Advertising				
Administrative costs				
Owner				
Professional staff				
Support staff				
Telephone				
Travel				
Supplies				

WORKSHEET #32 — Continued

	Quarter			
	First	Second	Third	Fourth
Sales expenditures				
Salaries and benefits				
Telephone				
Travel				
Marketing research				
Salaries and benefits				
Computer time				
Telephone				
Travel				
Miscellaneous				

	Yes	No	Comment
1. Is the plan understood by all in the company?	❑	❑	_____
2. Are the strategies of the plan coordinated with all aspects of the business (e.g., production, etc.)?	❑	❑	_____
3. Is the plan consistent with internal strengths, objectives, and policies?	❑	❑	_____
4. Is your organization's structure consistent with the plan?	❑	❑	_____
5. Is the plan acceptable to the major constituents of the company?	❑	❑	_____
6. Does the plan identify the primary unique characteristics of the business?	❑	❑	_____
7. Are your plan's marketing activities prioritized?	❑	❑	_____
8. Do you have or can your company get sufficient capital to implement the plan?	❑	❑	_____
9. Will this plan pit you against a powerful competitor?	❑	❑	_____
10. Have you made an honest, accurate appraisal of the competition?	❑	❑	_____
11. Particularly, have you underestimated the competition?	❑	❑	_____
12. Is the timing of the plan implementation appropriate given market conditions?	❑	❑	_____

13

IMPLEMENTING THE MARKETING ACTION PLAN

a. CONTROLLING IMPLEMENTATION

Your action plan puts your long anticipated marketing program in place. But you must ensure the plan is enacted. Establish a control system to tell you whether the marketing you have planned for your service business or professional practice is being accomplished on schedule.

Planning and implementing a control system will test the employees who perform each marketing task. You will demand powerful personal qualities, such as devotion, dedication, and faith, from them. But controls are set in place to assure the progress of your marketing plan; they control the work, not the people who do the work. Properly applied, controls can be an inspiration to those accomplishing the work, for controls provide clarity, direction, and feelings of achievement. And they will test your ability to lead your employees toward accomplishing each goal. If you are a one-person business, your control system will test your self-discipline and determination.

b. SETTING A SCHEDULE

Plan your control system using the deadlines of the marketing plan. In the action plan, you identified dates on which you'll check back and complete assigned tasks. Using any technique that works for you, note those deadlines on your daily calendar, where you'll be sure to see them. Or, mark them on a full-fledged project chart, dating each task of each activity of each strategy. The chart will remind all team members of upcoming deadlines.

Whatever your system, remember to keep it simple. Fancy charts and complex staff reports do nothing to create new business and, in fact, detract energy from the real marketing task.

Controls work best when some quantity — a date or number — is applied as a goal for the action plan. With the quantitative goal, everyone's expectations are clarified. Without it, no one knows for sure whether they have succeeded. Undoubtedly, some dates and numbers will be changed as implementation progresses, but having set them in the beginning moves your project into action. And when each quantitative goal is accomplished, confidence and enthusiasm grows.

c. STAYING ON SCHEDULE

Two things seem to have the greatest impact on achieving strategies on schedule. The first is having a realistic time line for each independent strategy. Without giving up too much time or energy to each project, plan more conservative deadlines than you think will be necessary. A delay after long, careful planning may seem frustrating to the aggressive, results oriented, and optimistic business owner. Recognize, however, that unrealistic deadlines can be demoralizing.

The second thing that will help you stay on schedule is having a time line for each strategy that meshes with the others. Be certain that any strategies to be accomplished simultaneously by the same personnel are complementary (e.g., researching and writing, rather than researching and selling). Make certain that the timelines follow marketing logic; you can't, for example, develop a brochure when the target market is not yet decided.

d. DIFFERENT RESULTS THAN EXPECTED? BECOME AN M.D.

When a control system is set in place, you'll know if the results you're getting are those you planned. For example, you might have planned to increase contact with existing clients by 10%, and now you're finding your staff is swamped and is making only about one quarter of the contacts planned. Or, you anticipated attracting three new clients by the end of the quarter, you've only acquired one, and you just might lose an existing client.

Don't be tempted to give up, feeling that it's not working if you don't get fast results. It will be better for the future of your business if, in the face of such frustration, you learn yet another marketing skill — that of Marketing Diagnostician, M.D. Then, in the face of discrepancies in results, you'll be able to stop, think about your problem, and diagnose its causes.

Marketing diagnosis is less precise than medical diagnosis. As in medical diagnosis, the M.D. may not be able to answer every question; some results are simply beyond your control. Nevertheless, the process for diagnosing the reason for different results is clear. It starts with the step closest to implementation and, when necessary, works back to questioning the most fundamental decisions. If you were one of the decision makers, you will be doubly challenged to wear your M.D. hat and not just your service provider hat during diagnosis.

1. The diagnostic process

To diagnose an implementation problem, relieve yourself of the highly charged word *problem*. Approach it as a puzzle. Discuss the puzzle thoroughly in closed meetings with the people who actually do the work. Ask which parts of the marketing plan work and which don't. Recognize that, in times of confusion, people respond with varying degrees of honesty. Back up oral assessments of the puzzle by gathering its pieces: results, information, and memoranda.

Since you are wearing the hats of both the M.D. and the service provider whose money is on the line, make a special effort to stay calm during diagnosis. Stress reduces the ability to take effective action.

Give your creative self an opportunity to work on the puzzle by relegating it to your subconscious and trying to relax. Let your subconscious ponder what the fundamental issue is, not who is to blame for it. Look at what should be done differently rather than merely restating the problem.

Ultimately, ask yourself the following questions:

- Is the way you're implementing the strategy at fault? For example, did you rely too much on referrals from previous clients? Perhaps you should pursue referrals from other sources more actively as well.

- Did you make an error in the plan itself? For example, did you choose too many target groups which, in retrospect, could have been the wrong marketing strategy? Instead, you could focus on key target groups and serve them well.

- If the plan is sound, were the original objectives as set by management valid? For example, should you have set an objective of increasing market share by 20% in a new area? Perhaps you should increase market share within one target market by 30% and plan to introduce your services to a new market by the end of the year.

2. Getting well again

Once you've identified the cause of the problem, cure it. Curing it may require simply changing the strategy or altering fundamental precepts on which decisions were made. In either instance, a change will require cooperation from all staff involved. Don't let foot-dragging happen. Face the need for change honestly. Then lead! Court, cajole, encourage, and restate the new objective until you're accused of being a broken record. Assisting staff through such change is one of those management challenges from which you'll inevitably grow.

As you implement your marketing plan, Worksheet #34 should help you clearly think through your problem, that is, your puzzle.

e. SYSTEMATIC MARKETING DIAGNOSIS

Although solving a single marketing problem requires considerable time, energy, and effort, ignore the temptation to forget the problem once it's corrected. Instead, remember that each strategy is related to others. Review other strategies and make the adjustments necessary to continue on the way to a successful marketing plan for your service business or professional practice.

1. What are the symptoms?

_____

_____

_____

_____

2. Why do you think there is a problem?

_____

_____

_____

_____

3. What investigation have you made to make this decision?

_____

_____

_____

_____

4. What results do you want instead? (Restate the objective.)

_____

_____

_____

_____

5. What strategy are you implementing now to get those results?

_____

_____

_____

6. What is your assessment of that implementation to date?

_____

_____

_____

_____

7. Did you originally set the right objective?

_____

_____

_____

_____

8. What are the possibilities? What could you do instead?

_____

_____

_____

_____

9. What corrective action should you take now?

_____

_____

_____

_____

OTHER TITLES IN THE SELF-COUNSEL BUSINESS SERIES

MARKETING YOUR PRODUCT
(with CD-ROM)

Donald Cyr and Douglas Gray
$18.95US/$24.95CDN
ISBN: 1-55180-394-1

- Plan for business success

- Get updated information on the Internet

- Develop the competitive edge

- Understand your customers

This marketing book is for the real world, not just the classroom. An informative planning guide that covers all the essentials, this newly updated and expanded edition demonstrates how to carve a niche for any product in today's competitive, fast-paced, and often fickle consumer environment.

Now including a chapter on the value of the Internet as a marketing tool, this long-trusted guide clearly explains common theories and provides step-by-step advice using plenty of helpful worksheets.

LOW BUDGET ON-LINE MARKETING FOR SMALL BUSINESS

Holly Berkley
$16.95US/$16.95CDN
ISBN: 1-55180-427-1

Large companies have huge budgets for marketing their products and services on-line. What's the difference between a $100,000 marketing campaign and a $1,000 campaign? Surprisingly, not much. This book teaches small-business operators how to achieve big-business marketing success on a small-business budget!

Low Budget On-Line Marketing for Small Business takes you behind the scenes of successful marketing campaigns. The book will show you how to cut costs so that you can adapt the successful marketing strategies of big companies for use in your business.

If you want to use the Web to attract attention, this book will show you how, and with only a minimal investment! Topics include —

- Targeting your campaign

- Generating free advertising

- E-mail marketing

- Building Web communities

- Successful co-branding strategies

- Banner advertising

- Web-design basics

- Search-engine registration

MARKET RESEARCH MADE EASY

Don Doman and Margaret Doman
$14.95US/$18.95CDN
ISBN: 1-55180-409-3

Market research is vital if you want to stay in touch with your industry and your customers.

Whether you are starting a new business, launching a product, setting a marketable price point, or simply trying to increase your market share, market research can tell you what you need to know.

A successful business cannot do without research.

The good news is, you can do it yourself. Market research is not the exclusive province of high-priced professionals. It is simply a process of asking questions or finding existing information about the market, your competition, and potential customers.

This practical, easy-to-read book has recently been expanded and updated. It answers questions such as —

- When should I do my market research?

- Where can I find the data I need?

- Who are my best survey subjects?

- How do I design a market-research questionnaire?

- Why should I use brainstorming sessions and focus groups in my research?

GETTING PUBLICITY

Tana Fletcher and Julia Rockler
$20.95US/$20.95CDN
ISBN: 1-55180-312-7

- Get publicity for your business, your organization, or yourself

- Master the essential media skills for success

- Learn practical tools for low-cost exposure

If you'd like to know all the inside secrets for attracting publicity to your business, your association, or yourself, you need this book. Step-by-step instructions illustrate just what it takes for any enterprise to generate media attention.

The authors, both award-winning journalists, show how you can make the most of every opportunity for free coverage in print, broadcast, and Internet media.

From newspaper articles to radio interviews, from television appearances to the World Wide Web, this expanded and updated edition includes all the advice you need to sparkle in the publicity spotlight.

Aimed specifically at individuals and organizations whose ambitions are bigger than their bankrolls, *Getting Publicity* emphasizes low-cost, do-it-yourself promotional strategies and is filled with inexpensive and practical tips for capitalizing on the power of publicity.

Includes —
- Becoming your own publicist
- Putting together a publicity plan
- Creating publicity opportunities
- Understanding the media
- Preparing publicity materials

BUSINESS WRITING BASICS

Jane Watson
$9.95US/$12.95CDN
ISBN: 1-55180-386-0

- Plan and write effective reports

- Create professional letters, memos, and e-mail

- Enhance the image of your business

Impress clients, colleagues, and even the boss with effective business-writing skills.

While a poorly written letter can embarrass an organization, a professionally penned document will enhance the image of both the company and the writer.

Containing more than 200 useful tips, *Business Writing Basics* will enhance your writing skills overnight. Read how you can —

- Add personality to your writing

- Avoid writer's block

- Plan and write reports

- Replace clichés and other antiquated phrases

- Use verbs that create powerful messages

- Create effective e-mail, faxes, letters, and memos

- Ensure your writing is read and produces the response you want

ORDER FORM

All prices are subject to change without notice. Books are available in book, department, and stationery stores. If you cannot buy the book through a store, please use this order form. (Please print.)

Name _____

Address _____

Charge to: ❏ Visa ❏ MasterCard

Account number_____

Validation date _____

Expiry date _____

Signature _____

YES, please send me:

____ *Marketing Your Product (with CD-ROM)*

____ *Low Budget On-Line Marketing for Small Business*

____ *Market Research Made Easy*

____ *Getting Publicity*

____ *Business Writing Basics*

Please add $4.95 for postage and handling.

Canadian residents, please add 7% GST to your order.

WA residents, please add 7.8% sales tax.

❏ Check here for a free catalog.

IN CANADA

Please send your order to the nearest location:

Self-Counsel Press
1481 Charlotte Road
North Vancouver, BC,
V7J 1H1

Self-Counsel Press
4 Bram Court
Brampton, ON,
L6W 3R6

IN THE USA

Please send your order to:

Self-Counsel Press Inc.
1704 N. State Street
Bellingham, WA 98225

Visit our Internet Web Site at
<www.self-counsel.com>.